F

To Frank, Timothy, Jeremy,
and their partners

Pamper Your Partner

PENNY RICH

Special photography by John Cocking

A FIRESIDE BOOK
PUBLISHED BY SIMON & SCHUSTER INC.
NEW YORK LONDON TORONTO SYDNEY TOKYO SINGAPORE

Editor LINDA BURROUGHS
Designer SANDRA HORTH
Production Controllers CLAIRE KANE AND JANET SLATER
Special photography JOHN COCKING
Stylist MANDY D'WITT
Hair and make-up SIONA

F FIRESIDE
Simon & Schuster Building
Rockefeller Center
1230 Avenue of the Americas
New York, New York 10020

First published in Great Britain
by the Hamlyn Publishing Group Limited,
a division of the Octopus Publishing Group,
Michelin House, 81 Fulham Road, London SW3 6RB.

Produced by Mandarin Offset – printed in Hong Kong.

10 9 8 7 6 5 4 3 2 1

Library of Congress Cataloging in Publication Data

Rich, Penny.
    Pamper your partner / Penny Rich.
        p.   cm.
    "A Fireside book."
    "First published in Great Britain by Hamlyn Publishing Group
Limited"—T.p. verso.
    ISBN 0-671-69526-6
    1. Sex customs.   2. Massage.   3. Sex in marriage.   I. Title.
HQ16.R53   1990
613.9'6—dc20   89-25842
                                                    CIP

AUTHOR'S ACKNOWLEDGMENTS
Thanks to: Vivien Long (trained in
shiatsu, aromatherapy, and traditional
Thai and Swedish massage) for her advice
and help with the four massage programs,
and for rubbing away my writer's cramp
at the end of each week; Anita and Barry
Phillips (between them, a lawyer,
aromatherapist and organizers of the
Essential Oil Traders Association in the
UK) for their commonsense comments on
the second chapter; the exclusive Lambton
Place Health Club, London W2, England,
for letting me use their gym instructor,
Karin Hoare, to work on, and work-out
on, the three exercise programs in the final
chapter; my US connections, Joanna
Brown and Lesley Cunliffe, plus Annette
Green of The Fragrance Foundation, New
York; my editor, Linda Burroughs, for
being there (and being calm, cool, and
collected).

PUBLISHER'S
ACKNOWLEDGMENTS
The publishers would like to thank the
following for permission to reproduce the
photographs: James Murphy 51, 66–7;
P.W.A. 91, 106–7, 108; Simon Wheeler 57,
61; World Press Network 81.
The publishers would like to thank the
following for the loan of properties for
photographs: Debenhams – towel 18;
Hennes – girl's T shirt 16, girl's shirt 46,
girl's shirt 47, girl's top 49; man's Levis 86,
man's belt 117, girl's top 126; Marks and
Spencer – boxer shorts 16, vests 18, vests
19, vests 54, man's vest 68–9, man's vest
86, man's vest 89, girl's vest 119, man's vest
120, vests 121, vests 122, vests 123, man's
vest 126; Mexx at Harrods, Liberty,
Selfridges – man's shirt and waistcoat 75,
man's shirt 111, man's jacket and shirt
114, man's shirt and trousers 117; Next –
towel 49; Pineapple (mail order available),
6A Langley Street, Covent Garden,
London WC2 H9JA (tel: 01-497-2799) –
girl's top 32, girl's top 61, girl's top and
leggings 89, dress 111, dress 114, girl's top
120, cycle shorts 126, girl's top 128, girl's
top 131.

Contents

The *loving* touch 8

Reach out and rub • The miracle of massage • Rubbing up the right way • The oil slick • Rhythm and clues • When not to massage • Massage and childbirth • Going through the motions • The basic strokes • Four step-by-step massages • The neck, face, and scalp massage • The back massage • The foot massage • The sensual body massage

Scents *and* sensuality 50

Winning by a nose • Aromatherapy: the sensual science • Down to the essentials • The common scents of smell • Do-it-yourself aromatherapy • The aromatic touch • Matching mood and massage • The aromatic smell • A fresh approach • The top 20 home treats • Down to a tea

Water *and* well *being* 82

On the water front • Spa-ing partners • Bathtime basics • Essential aquatherapy • The rub-a-dub-tub • Soft soaping your partner • Taking the plunge • The water works • The bath plugger

Time *for* together*ness* 110

The stress factor • Close encounters of the absurd kind • The flip side of stress • Six high-pressure points • Six power pushes • Six tension busters • Playing footsie • Digital delights • The magical manicure • The pampering pedicure • The air lift • The best sleeping potion

Glossary *of* further *techniques* 141

Useful *addresses* 142

Index 144

This *book* is *for* couples

It contains dozens of simple techniques for pampering your partner – whether that person is your lover, spouse, friend, or roommate. The word 'partner' is every bit as important as the word 'pamper', because looking after someone you care about is one of the greatest pleasures in life. It strengthens your relationship and emotional bonds, recharges tired minds and tense bodies, and gives you a moment of intimate escape from the pressures of the world.

It is twice as pleasurable if your partner also pampers you. Smothering your tired body with a pot of Chanel No 5 moisturizing cream soothes on the surface; having someone to rub it in for you penetrates deeper than any cream or potion used alone. Everyone benefits from the loving touch: executives who need to switch off, insomniacs who crave sleep, mothers who need energy, couples who aren't communicating, students under pressure, and lovers who lack sensuality. Anyone who is tired and jaded at the end of a demanding and stressful day – whether they spent it sitting on a tractor in a field, or at a computer in the city – needs to relax, repair, and recharge for whatever tomorrow has in store.

As our daily lives become more stressful, this need is even greater. Research now proves that stress and sickness go hand in hand, and that relaxation is vital for our physical well-being. But the aim of this book is to go deeper than that. By taking time out to relax *together*, to adore, spoil, and care for one another, you are treating the whole self. Being pampered by the person closest to you brings you closer to him or her, so that you unburden the emotional and mental load as much as you relieve the aches and strains of world-weary muscles.

There are two senses that we have less time to enjoy now, than ever before – touch and smell. They are primitive, potent, intimate ways of communicating, and so each has as entire section in this book (massage and aromatherapy, covered in the first two chapters). The treats and treatments included in the other two chapters – from soaking in a warm bath to physically stretching out stress with exercises – have been chosen because they are simple, speedy routines that slot into any lifestyle, and instantly make life better.

How much pleasure you get from this book depends on how much time you put aside to spend together. The choice is yours. The treatments all combine, and may be mixed and matched from every page. In only ten minutes you can touch the Six High Pressure Points which wipe away tension from the base of the shoulders to the top of the head: double the time and you can soothe the psyche (and the soles) with the deeply relaxing Foot Massage. And from here on, the more time you add only adds to the pleasure. The only thing you shouldn't do, is hold the book in one hand while you practise with the other. Trust your instincts, throw in your own special touches, and look to your partner's real needs – that is what pampering is all about.

The *loving* touch is worth a thousand words.

Skin on skin is a potent way of communicating. Even a quick, formal handshake speaks volumes. In a few seconds we subconsciously decide if we are making contact with a friend or enemy – firm or weak grip, damp or cool skin, negative or positive signals, are all registered from a mere five square inches of physical contact. And when we increase the area of contact, we dramatically increase the power of touch.

A hurried hug puts us at ease; five minutes of close cuddling leaves us soothed, calm, comforted, and relaxed; and a lifetime of touch makes us feel loved, secure, happy, and healthy. But although touch is the first of the five senses a child develops in the womb, it is the first we lose as we grow up. We never outgrow the need; society just makes it harder to satisfy. Babies register all pleasure and pain through touch, but as adolescents we know not to run crying to Mother for cuddles when we hurt. And by the time we are adults, we have learned to minimize casual physical contact – on the street, in trains, on buses, in shopping malls, we don't even make eye contact with strangers let alone body contact. Even in our everyday lives we end up

The feel of skin on skin satisfies deep emotional needs and makes us happier and healthier throughout our lives.

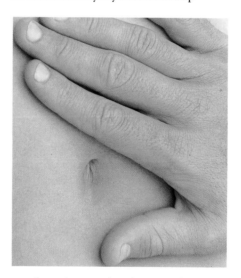

touching things rather than people 80 percent of the time – buttons on machines, appliances, the telephone, and hundreds of other modern devices.

Repressing casual touch between people is something that is peculiar to the developed Western world, especially among town or city dwellers. Eskimos and Maoris still greet strangers by pressing or rubbing noses, which is far more intimate than a handshake. In Africa, India or China, villagers gather round to touch a stranger. And even native cultures that have been absorbed into the twentieth century – like the Aborigines or North

American Indians – are less conditioned than we are to avoid physical contact. The British are renowned for their reticence in touching other people; Americans are generally more extrovert and slightly less inhibited with strangers; but it is only continental Europeans who are still not frightened to walk arm in arm down the street or kiss on meeting.

In modern society, touching an on/off button more frequently than touching another finger is a fact of life. But it affects us, indirectly, far more than we realize. By losing out on casual human contact we have an even greater need for intimate touch. Scientific research has established that this need is both physical and emotional, and that it is constant throughout our lives. Although you can't kill someone with kindness, lack of affection can be fatal. As far back as the turn of the century, doctors investigating the high mortality rate in orphanages isolated a disease called Marasmus. It seemed that what these babies were suffering from in an institutionalized system was lack of love and physical touch to the extent that they died from no other cause. More recently, research on geriatric wards in hospitals has shown that the elderly respond miraculously to a daily dose of cuddles – their memories improve, they become more gregarious, and many of the outward signs of senility disappear. Touch therapy is now recognized as important in all areas – patients in hospital recover quicker from surgery, the handicapped learn faster, and the emotionally disturbed respond to psychiatric treatment more positively.

Touching is also vital in early life – physically it makes us grow taller and have a healthier immune system; emotionally it gives us the confidence and character to cope with adulthood. But the real power of touch is pure pleasure. Pressing skin against skin is sensual. It is a way of communicating that keeps us sane in a mad world. It makes us love ourselves and grow closer to other people. It saves marriages, and wipes away worries.

Reach out and rub

Massage is the simplest and most sensual way to satisfy our desire to touch and be touched. It is more gratifying than all the casual pats, strokes, hugs, tickles, squeezes, and caresses that we receive in day-to-day life – just as eating a fresh orange is more enjoyable than swallowing a vitamin C tablet. It is a tactile, tender, intimate, and intense form of touch. And it soothes both the body and the mind, so that you feel better in minutes – not days, weeks, or months. When you reach out and rub your hands over your partner's body you rub away tension, pain, grumpiness and anxiety – the pressure of hands banishes the pressures of life.

The added pleasure of massage is that it is as much fun to give as it is to receive. It offers the chance to explore and learn about every contour of your partner's body, the lumps and the bumps, the texture and the feel of the skin. This creates a new sensual intimacy, which is completely different from the old sexual one. In fact, as Masters and Johnson have shown in their studies of human sexuality, touch as a means of sensual awareness is just as rewarding and important as the mad-rush-to-orgasm (otherwise known as intercourse). Counsellors and analysts throughout the world advise couples to touch each other more – and many believe

Massage is a potent form of touch that lets you and your partner communicate in the tenderest, most tactile, and intimate way.

that the rising divorce rate could be caused by lack of physical contact within families.

The pleasure of massage has been valued for centuries, and ancient Chinese, Egyptian, Indian, Greek, and Roman cultures all succumbed. Over 2,500 years ago, Hippocrates – the father figure of modern medicine – gave rubbing his vote of approval for both its pampering and healing benefits. Roman gladiators used it to prepare themselves for the rigours of wrestling with lions, and Roman emperors included it as the prime party game at orgies. Louis XV never left Versailles without his masseur in tow. And Captain Cook found it almost impossible to leave the Pacific, once he discovered the delights of being massaged by Tahitian women.

By the late eighteenth century the word had spread to health spas throughout Europe – thanks mainly to Per Henrik

Ling, who invented a rubbing technique called Swedish massage, based on his knowledge of gymnastics and physiology and from what he had seen while travelling in the East. For the first time massage thrived in the modern world and was practised by medics for its therapeutic and pleasurable properties. But the Victorians put a stop to all that a hundred years later. They decided touch was taboo, and anything sensual was a sin;

they became so embroiled in the Industrial Revolution that even marble statues were draped with fabric to hide their private parts. Massage was allowed only if you were injured or unwell and were seeking a cure. As a therapy, it survived until World War II, to treat wounded or shell-shocked soldiers.

Within a decade, the miracle of modern medicine pushed massage even further into the doldrums. New pain-killing drugs

The physical, psychological, and sheer sensual pleasure of skin touching skin has always been enjoyed instinctually, as part of the bond between loving couples.

meant that a single pill could knock out the entire nervous system and cure a headache – and busy doctors could treat aches or anxieties with a simple prescription. Massage took on a purely pleasurable role and was enjoyed by hippies on the beach or wealthy women at the beauticians. Suddenly it was an esoteric therapy, and those in the know talked of shiatsu, reflexology, aromatherapy – and massage's many other guises (see Glossary on page 141).

But in the last 30 years, as researchers have discovered more about how the human body functions, treating the cause of illness has become as important as treating the symptoms. And drugs are not the final answer. By looking at the body as a whole – physically and emotionally – medics have made some astounding breakthroughs in understanding what makes us tick. This new knowledge means that for the first time since Stone Age man patted his pet baby dinosaur, we know why touch makes us tick better.

The miracle of massage

It is a natural human instinct to rub away pain. Without thinking, we automatically hold our stomachs when they ache, rub a bumped elbow, or touch our temples with a fingertip when we have a headache. Massage is simply a development of this instinct – but we now realize it has sound physiological grounding.

Research into pain control has shown that rubbing is one of the body's natural pain-blocking processes. When we rub the skin we stimulate touch receptors which send impulses to the brain via what scientists call a 'gate' in the spinal chord – and as touch impulses travel faster than pain, by the time the pain reaches the gate, it has already closed. In effect, rubbing an area that hurts stops the pain message getting through. This works on a simple level to soothe stiff necks, back ache or bumps and knocks. But prolonged or intense pain eventually beats down the

Rubbing the body when it hurts wipes away pain temporarily, by blocking the message as it travels to the brain, and replacing the hurt with the feeling of pleasant touch.

gate, and rubbing can't short circuit the message system indefinitely.

Human skin registers dozens of sensations through millions of receptors all over the two square yards of its body surface. They are so sensitive that they tell us the difference between a kitten's fluffy fur or the slimy surface of a worm – and they can register feeling when 0.0002 of an inch of skin is indented for one tenth of a second. We have more touch receptors in our hands and feet than any other area of the body, which is the main reason that using hands to give a massage is such unadulterated pleasure.

Recent research at Yale University and the Harvard Medical School has shown a possible new function of human skin. It used to be thought that the epidermis's main role was as a sensitive and protective wrapper for the body. Now scientists have discovered that skin is a biochemical organ with cells that interact to produce or remodel hormones, enzymes, and other substances that are important to our immune system. This interaction can be triggered by external stimuli, such as light, chemicals, microbes and friction. So massage may not only be fun, it may also be good for you.

The physical benefits of a good massage have been recorded for thousands of years. It helps soothe strains and pains, anxiety and stress. It can put an insomniac to sleep or give the lethargic a burst of instant energy. And we now know it can do any of these things without the side effects we get from an analgesic, barbiturate, or amphetamine. More recent research has also shown exactly how massage works on the vascular and muscular systems.

The vascular system is made up of the vessels that supply blood and lymph fluid throughout the body. Blood delivers fresh oxygen and lymph removes bacteria, toxins, and other wastes that build up in tissues. When you have a massage, the movement of blood from the heart to the extremities and back again is speeded up – after five minutes, the oxygen content of all rubbed tissue has increased ten to 15

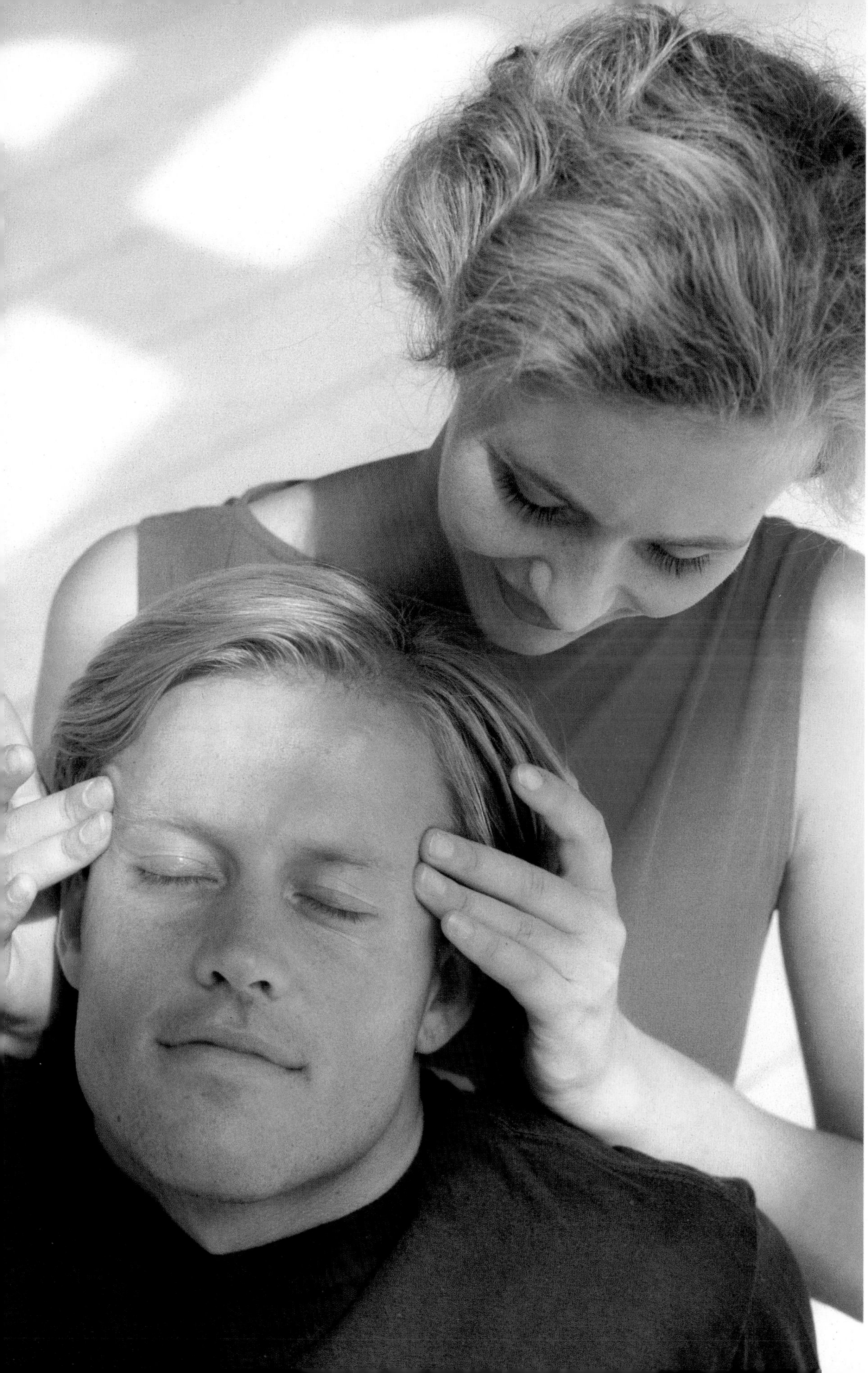

The *loving* touch

percent. But blood pressure actually drops because the masseur's hands take over some of the pushing done by the heart as it beats. So you have improved circulation with less effort from the body itself. The lymph, which filters wastes through nodes in the neck, armpits, groin, and behind the knees, only circulates by compression of muscles and the suction created by every breath we take. It is not very efficient, and wastes often build up when the system is sluggish, but massage encourages lymphatic drainage.

The muscular system responds to massage in a similar way, but to overcome a very different problem. When we are tense or worried our muscles automatically tighten – think of a frown, which we often don't even know is crowning our forehead. Since the world is full of worries, from meeting a deadline to missing another car that is coming towards us, our bodies are constantly reacting. The result of this is that stress is not purely mental – it affects our bodies physically, and accumulates so that tight muscles stay contracted for long periods of time. This stops waste products moving out of muscles, and lactic acid builds up so the area is stiff, sore and painful when touched. And it's a vicious cycle, because waste products cause tension and tension produces more wastes. But massage makes the muscles let go and stimulates cleansing quicker than if the wastes were just left to disperse naturally.

Lactic acid also builds up when muscles are exercised vigorously; athletes are still only human and reach pain barriers beyond which they cannot physically go. A lot of research has been carried out in the field of endurance – mainly because sport is so competitive these days – and it has shown that muscle recovery rates are greatly increased with massage. If an athlete does 100 sit-ups, then rests for five minutes, and can then do a further 20 sit-ups, he has an average recovery rate (20 percent). But clinical tests prove that with five minutes of massage instead of rest, the same person is able to manage an

additional 120 sit-ups – a recovery rate five times better than normal. This is why massage is now included in almost all sports training worldwide and why you see athletes being rubbed up the right way from the Olympics to the local track.

The real miracle of massage is that something as simple as rubbing skin against skin can have such astonishing repercussions. It pampers both the body and mind and lets you grow closer to your partner at the same time. It cleanses the body, stimulates the circulation, comforts, and consoles. It relieves aches and pains, anxiety and stress. And it leaves you feeling healthier, happier, and with a more positive attitude to both yourself and others. It is one of the few forms of touch that is non-threatening and non-sexual, yet still satisfying when received from a total stranger. And when it is enjoyed by you and your partner jointly, it is doubly satisfying and very sensual.

When you consider all the plus points of indulging in a massage, the only question that remains unanswered is why it is not taught alongside mathematics or spelling! But since it isn't, many of us feel frightened of not being able to do it properly. The first rule of massage is to trust your intuition. Feel, don't think. It should be simplified to something that is so natural that you make it up using the basic strokes as you go along. Balancing an open book beside you as you try to follow it stage by stage defeats the issue and gives you brain strain. It's not much fun for your partner either, and you'll both end up wishing you'd gone to the movies instead.

Learning how to enjoy a massage is almost as important as having one in the first place. There is nothing more delightful than giving pleasure so easily to someone you care about. So always concentrate on the loving touch. Be kind, caring, calm, and gentle. If you've had a hard day and are not in the mood, then turn to another chapter in the book and choose an alternative way of pampering your partner. This is massage, not wrestling – for pleasure, not pain.

Good sports include massage in any fitness programme, from amateur to professional, because it releases extra muscle energy and increases performance levels.

Rubbing up the right way

In order to enjoy any massage, you both have to be relaxed, warm, and comfortable. Retreating from the world will help you retreat from its demands and pressures. So choose the most peaceful room in the house where you won't be disturbed. Take the phone off the hook, dim the lights so the whole procedure is more sensual and sleepy, and make sure the room is comfortably warm before you start. Once you feel cold, your muscles automatically contract with goose bumps and shivers – which means you can't relax properly. A hot bath beforehand not only will raise your body temperature, but will loosen muscles and help you absorb oil more readily during the massage (for extra

bathtime treats, tricks and techniques, turn to Water and well-being). And to keep him or her snug throughout, cover your partner with a layer of towels, and fold them back as you go, so that only the area you're massaging is exposed.

The best place to do a massage is on top of a table or on the floor. You need a firm, padded surface so that the pressure you exert is absorbed by the body alone. Most beds are too soft and end up acting like a trampoline. However, if your partner is very tired and you're giving a gentle, stroking massage to help him drift off to sleep, bed is the only place to start. If you're using a table top, make sure it is about thigh height so you can bend and reach without straining your back. If you're massaging on the floor, you'll be

resting on your knees and will need a cushion to kneel on. And for either surface, you'll need to throw down a couple of thick blankets, a padded quilt or a foam sheet to cushion the body you're working on.

Your partner will probably appreciate a little extra padding to help her relax totally: when she is face up, slip a small cushion under the knees (to reduce the arch of the lower back) and a folded towel under the head (to raise it about an inch and release shoulder muscles); when she is face down, use a rolled towel under the ankles (to relax the back) and a cushion under the waist (to straighten the spine). And so you are relaxed while giving a massage, wear comfortable, loose-fitting clothes – not too many layers, though,

because you'll soon warm up from the exercise. A half hour spent rubbing, stroking, and pummelling your partner's body has the bonus of working out a few muscles you might not have used recently yourself. When it comes to massage, giving isn't necessarily easier than receiving. But if you make sure you're always facing in the direction of your strokes you won't hurt or twist your neck. Keep your back straight for the same reason, and with practice you'll learn to work without tensing your own muscles.

Improvise as you go along and let comfort and convenience be your guide. For instance, you can give a great back massage if you sit your partner on a stool and let his head rest forward onto pillows on a table top. This stretches out the part

While warming up for a massage, remember to throw in the towels: they are the best padding for a relaxed position and can be draped over exposed skin to prevent it getting cold.

of the body you're working on so it's more receptive, and is ideal if you want to indulge in a bit of quick pampering when you're dressed for dinner and almost ready to run out the door. With practice, you'll soon find out which positions are most pleasurable for both you and your partner.

The same applies to getting in the mood. Some people swear by massaging in time to a Mozart concerto, while others prefer the sound of silence. Itchy types don't mind a bit of scratch with their rubbing, but the ticklish prefer neatly trimmed nails for a softer touch. As massage is all about skin on skin, it is worth remembering to take off all jewellery before you start. Try to let your hands do the talking and keep conversation to a minimum. A few minutes of peace and quiet can be more intimate and rewarding than an hour of foreplay. If your partner drifts off to sleep don't get cross and think she's not appreciating your touch – it is a sign of an excellent masseur or masseuse. And if he starts talking at the speed of sound, it means your partner is so relaxed that he's unburdening an emotional load as well as a physical one. Every massage is different and has a different effect, but all of them bring you closer than a thousand words on the same subject. When it comes to communicating, the massage itself is the main message you are trying to deliver.

The oil slick

Oil helps your hands glide over your partner's body in the most tactile, sensual way, but only if it has been warmed to body temperature before you begin the massage.

Oil helps you give a smooth, flowing massage by lubricating the skin so your hands glide over the surface without unnecessary friction. It also helps make it a more sensual, tactile experience. The best type is a light vegetable oil, either on its own or mixed with a scented essential oil (see Scents and sensuality, pages 62–73).

Avoid those that are thick and greasy and slow your hands, or have a heavy odour – such as olive, corn or peanut oil. The pleasantest oils to use are soya, safflower, grapeseed or sunflower. Or you can try coconut if you want to be reminded

of tropical holidays; sesame for its light, nutty smell; peach kernel for the smell of summer on a dark winter night; avocado, jojoba, or apricot kernel, which are particularly rich in vitamins A and E and soften hard, rough skin; or sweet almond, a slightly heavier oil with significant quantities of vitamins E and F.

Keep your oil in a glass bottle with a flip top and in-built pouring nozzle if possible, so it is easy to add a few drops during the massage but won't spill if you knock it over. A plastic container may taint the oil and change its smell.

If you pour oil straight onto a body, it's like dousing your partner with cold water. So always warm it first. The simplest way is to immerse the glass bottle in a bowl of hot water for a few minutes before you start. Or you can pour some into the palm of your hand and let your body heat warm it gradually. If your hands are cold, wash them in a basin of hot water. Dry them, then rub them vigorously together for a minute or two until they tingle. When you're ready to start, spread the oil slowly over the body area by stroking it on until you have enough for your hands to glide smoothly. The quantity varies from skin to skin, depending how dry it is, but it is better to use a little and build up rather than use too much and have to listen to squelching noises throughout.

Some people use talcum powder as a lubricant, but as it just sits on the surface of skin it is not nearly so therapeutic or sensual. It is a good alternative to oil if your partner has allergic or sensitive reactions to emollients. Ordinary body moisturizers are absorbed too quickly and are not tactile enough. But you can buy special massage lotions which are rich and lubricating enough to grease the skin for up to half an hour. They are good to use on those occasions when you want to get dressed after a massage without leaving an oil slick on your favourite underwear. However, if you learn to use just enough oil rather than too much, it should be completely absorbed by your partner's skin at the end of the massage.

The loving touch

Rhythm and clues Before you master the basic steps of any massage, there are a few guidelines to remember. Stroking is a natural instinct, so there is no point in trying to be too precise or pendantic about it. Just familiarize yourself with the sequence of movements, then follow your intuition. The real fun of massage is never doing the same procedure twice. If you experiment, a single stroke can be soothing or stimulating.

It depends on how you do it, and you can instantly alter your routine to suit the needs of the moment. Whether you follow a sequence exactly, or improvise totally, the following tips and suggestions will guarantee that every massage is as pleasurable as possible.

● Rhythm is vital. Without it you will work in fits and starts; with it you will automatically reassure, relax, and revitalize your partner. So make sure your hands move at the same pace while repeating the same movement. Let them flow, sweep, and soothe the skin, not jerk or stop-and-start sporadically. The rhythm will also help relax you, so that your breathing is slow and calming and you don't sound like a steam locomotive. Don't try too hard because it will only make you feel self-conscious. You don't have to hurry – it's not a race, so take your time. The more you massage, the easier it becomes to slip into your own natural rhythm.

● Constant contact means a massage is more sensual, tactile, and thrilling. It also makes the individual movements seem like one continuous, flowing touch. So even if you are changing positions, try to leave the palms of your hands on your partner's skin while you move. Even leaving one hand in place as you move around his body is better than breaking contact altogether and interrupting the

sense of constant motion. And don't be afraid to touch him with your body as you lean over for longer strokes. It all adds to the fun.

● Explore your partner's body and learn as you go along. You will soon be able to feel if muscles are tight (knotted and lumpy), if tissue is retaining fluid (soft, spongy and slack), or where there are pockets of tension (nodules and tiny hard crystals of lactic acid). You'll also find out which parts of her body are strong, sensitive, ticklish, tender, weak, or vulnerable. And you'll soon discover what type of touch she finds stimulating, calming, or erotic. Always start by exploring intuitively so that you feel, rather than think about, her needs. It makes it all much more intimate.

● You don't have to confine yourselves to the massages suggested here, nor do you have to follow every step. And don't forget the less obvious – often less glamorous – parts of the body, such as the fingers and the knees. Anyone who has spent a hard day at a computer keyboard or scribbling research notes will appreciate your taking the time to unknot the muscles in the forearm, fingers and back of the hand. Paradoxically, knees and ankles may ache because we sit down all day, or because we stand up all day. Even if there isn't time for a full foot massage, a little attention to these key areas goes a long way.

Keep in touch with your partner throughout the massage by leaving your hands resting sensuously on skin whenever you change position or start a new stroke.

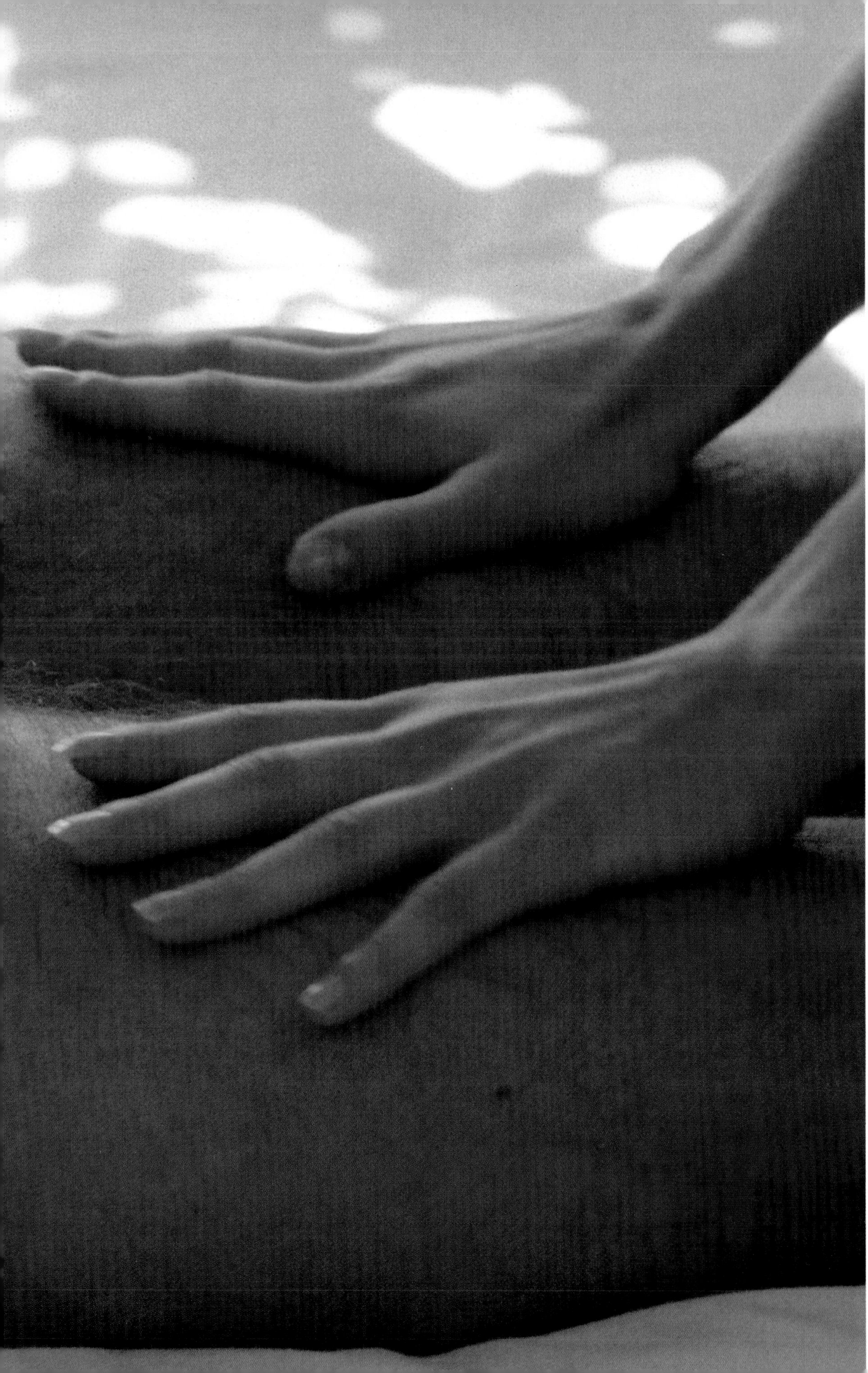

The *loving* touch

• Vary your touch by altering the speed or pressure of basic movements. A firm, brisk hand is invigorating, whereas soft, slow stroking can send your partner to sleep. Keep a light touch over bony places, but dig deeper into large muscles. And don't be afraid to use a strong hand with the weight of your body behind it – this just increases the pressure of your stroke, and it feels marvellous on very tense muscles. But the best way to get rid of very lumpy or knotted areas is to touch them firmly but briefly, then go back later again and again until you ease the tension out. Massage should never be painful, and if you discover a tender patch, remember where it is so you can use a lighter touch.

• Repetition is more relaxing than variety, so don't be frightened to repeat the same movement hundreds of times – that is what gradually releases body tension. It is the opposite of exercise, where too many repeats lead to pain. With massage, the more you rub, the better it feels. Try to remember to pace yourself and not chop and change strokes as if you are racing to the finish line; otherwise you'll destroy the hypnotic mood you are working to create. If your partner doesn't like what you are doing you'll soon know, but you often have to encourage him to grunt some kind of approval so you can give him enough of his favourite strokes.

• Let your fingers guide you as much as your eyes – if not more. Mould your hands to the contours and outlines of your partner's body. Never force skin or muscles into unnatural or strained positions, and take care around bony areas. Never massage or press directly on the vertebrae along the spine.

• While tickling can be good therapy (see page 116), ticklishness can be a serious impediment to a good massage. It is often the result of nervous tension, and you will only make matters worse if you persist with the same stroke over the ticklish area. Move your hands to just outside the ticklish zone and increase the pressure very slightly. Continue massaging until you are sure that this surrounding area is completely relaxed. Gradually extend the movement, keeping up the pressure, until the original area is incorporated in the complete stroke. By this time, it will almost certainly have stopped being uncomfortably ticklish.

• Relax and enjoy giving the massage. If you're calm, confident, and happy you'll use a loving touch, and your partner will feel it in the most sensual, sensitive way – through her skin. But be warned: the pure pleasure of being rubbed can be addictive and eventually a time will come when your partner wants to indulge and you don't. Since pampering only works if it is reciprocal, you should both try something from another chapter in the book first. Perhaps the relaxing body presses (see pages 120–131) or a stimulating aromatherapy bath (on page 97) will put you in a more positive mood, and the massage may follow naturally. The same approach should apply to how long it lasts; whether you rub your partner for ten minutes or an hour will depend on how you both feel at the time. There are no rules – pleasure is a natural alarm clock.

When not to massage

Even if you're in the mood and both parties are over the age of consent, there are some occasions when massage isn't recommended. Always consult your doctor before you massage someone who has any of the following conditions:

● an infection, a fever, high temperature, or a contagious disease;

● recent surgery, broken bone, open wound or swelling;

● a skin eruption, such as acne, eczema or heat rash;

● a heart condition, varicose veins, or other circulatory problems;

● a history of back problems or acute back pain.

The main reason you shouldn't massage anyone suffering from any of these conditions is that it stirs up both the lymph and blood flow throughout the body. So if someone is unwell, it may spread infection to surrounding tissues or make him feel wobbly and worse than before. You can relieve bad back pain by gently stroking and soothing the area, but never exert pressure or massage vigorously. Massaging the hands and feet can spread a feeling of general well-being throughout the body.

Massage and childbirth

A careful, gentle massage often helps during pregnancy. It not only soothes the mother, but also quietens those babies that are intent on early football practice. But again, you should check with your doctor before you start. Concentrate mainly on the legs, abdomen, and back, as these are the parts of an expectant mother's body that bear the brunt of the baby's weight. The most comfortable massage positions during pregnancy depend on your size, but as you get bigger it becomes more difficult. For a leg or abdomen massage, try lying back against a pile of cushions so you are half propped up, or lie flat with a small cushion under your spine to relax the lower back muscles. To work from the waist to the shoulders, either lie on your side, or sit astride a chair, facing the back, and lean forward onto a pillow draped over the chairback. And throughout the massage your partner should use smooth, gentle, soothing movements.

During labour, massage is a good way for a father-to-be to make a positive contribution and be physically involved. Relieve backache by gently rubbing the back, shoulders and neck with light, smooth, and flowing movements. Firmer pressure on the base of the spine and the buttocks can relieve lower back pain, but do not use deep pressure strokes elsewhere on the torso. Do not massage the abdomen. Massaging the feet also relieves pain and tension. Concentrate on the soles, where you can apply deep pressure. Be guided by your partner – she knows what is most comforting.

It is important for a woman to rest fully between contractions. Gently stroking her face may be reassuring and soothing, and helps to release tension, but don't try to do a full face, neck, and scalp massage.

There is probably no time in a woman's life when she is more in need of pampering than after childbirth. Gently massaging her abdomen will encourage uterine contraction, relax tense and overtired muscles, and counteract the nervous strain that many new mothers feel. Perhaps even more important, it is a way of being intimate, loving, and sensual without being sexual. Check with the obstetrician before starting a regular massage routine. Keep to gentle, flowing movements, and always stop if your partner complains of discomfort. Never massage directly on a Caesarean scar.

Going through the motions

Basic massage strokes can be grouped into three main categories: light pressure, which uses the hands and fingers in gentle sweeps; medium pressure, which penetrates deeper into tissue and uses the thumbs and fingers more; and deep pressure, which helps stimulate the circulation, cleanse the body and release tension.

The greatest pleasure of massage is never doing the same routine twice: so always improvise, experiment, throw in your own special touches, and learn to feel your partner's needs.

Some you'll adore and others you'll hate, but remember that you can completely change the feeling of each movement by slightly altering the speed and pressure. The lightest touch can become a deep stroke just by increasing the push power. After you've familiarized yourself with the individual movements, practise them on your leg or abdomen so you know the different sensations they give. Then do each one quickly and slowly, firmly and softly, until you've worked out all the permutations. Once you've mastered this, you can begin to improvise and use them in a variety of different ways and combinations to develop your own personal style. And this is how the best massages evolve, through feeling instinctually your partner's needs and giving her pleasure while enjoying it yourself every step of the way.

Always start a massage slowly, using soft, broad, gentle sweeps to spread the oil. Build up to more rhythmic, gliding strokes so that the flowing, unbroken motion starts to relax your partner. Then gradually add some of the medium and deep pressure techniques. These are best used sparingly, but repeated time and time again, with lighter, longer, more soothing strokes interspersed to increase the pleasure. Throughout any massage, you'll find you use light pressure strokes most – try to return instinctively to them whenever you're not sure what to do next. They are calming, warming, and relaxing, and keep up the body contact that makes massage so delightful. They can also be used anywhere on the body by just altering the length of the stroke.

Medium pressure techniques can be adapted and used pretty well all over to start to relax muscles. But the deeper pressure techniques are best on fleshy or well-muscled areas where real tension builds up. The vigorous deep pressure techniques – such as chopping with the sides of rigid hands, knuckling, pummelling with the fists, or slapping with the palm down – have deliberately been left out because they are often not very relaxing. They can also be dangerous in the hands of beginners. An over-enthusiastic masseur can make you feel as if you've done ten rounds with Mike Tyson until he learns to moderate his force factor. They are not particularly conducive to intimacy, sensuality or total relaxation – which is the aim of this book.

If you ever need to adapt one of the massages given here so that it is invigorating and stimulating rather than soothing and calming, it is safer just to increase the speed of any of the basic movements. Or you can try simple friction in combination with basic strokes; move your hands quickly and firmly in the same or opposite directions (like a fast rub), circle the palms, rake the fingertips, or do longer sweeps at a very fast pace. This warms and loosens muscles and improves the circulation by making blood rush to the skin surface so your partner feels wide awake, full of energy, but stress free.

Finally, you should remember always to face in the direction of the stroke that you are doing. This is the only way you can relax yourself and instantly add the push of your body weight if you want a firmer touch. If you are massaging on the floor,

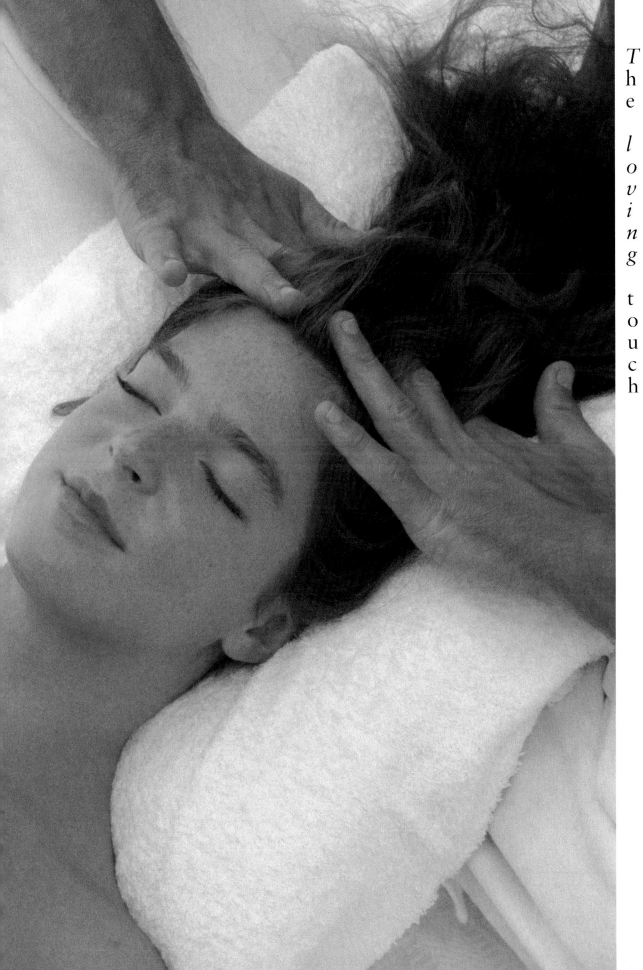

you'll find you move around your partner instinctively as you get into the rhythm. You can sit on the floor, kneel beside or over him and straddle his thighs to change the length or direction of strokes. If he is lying on a table, again you'll quickly find the most natural position to deliver different movements. Just don't think about it too much.

The basic strokes

The 12 basic strokes shown here have been placed in groups of light, medium, and deep pressure. However, the degree of pressure you exert on each one is a matter of personal taste – yours and your partner's. For example, raking, described here as a medium pressure stroke, becomes a different kind of movement if you apply your hands more lightly. Experiment on yourself and your partner to find out what suits you both best.

LIGHT PRESSURE

STROKING is the simplest movement in massage, and you should use it often, all over the body. Let one hand follow after the other as you would stroke a pet. It is a light, flowing movement that you can do in a downward or upward motion.

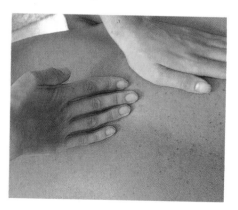

For variations, run hands in the same direction but moving about three inches apart on larger body areas (the length of the back, along the limbs). Or you can alternate the hands so that one is moving upward while the other is moving downward. It is an extremely relaxing, sensual touch.

FANNING is started with your hands a couple of inches apart, palms down and fingers together, pointing in the direction of the stroke. Glide your hands over the skin with even pressure, and when you've gone as far as you wish, spread your hands outwards in opposite directions (like a fan opening wide). Pull the skin back as you draw hands down to the start position. Keep the initial strokes short, then gradually make them longer as you repeat the movement.

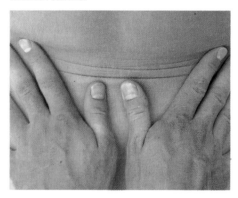

For variation, do the same basic stroke on the entire back, but give it a twist at the end: once your hands have gone up and fanned out over the shoulders, draw them down the sides as far as the waist, then into the middle of the lower back, cross them over and continue down the hips and back round the buttocks. This just alters the basic stroke so that you end up doing a large figure eight shape on the torso.

CIRCLING involves keeping your palms flat and fingers together. Make small firm circling movements with your hands, working in opposite directions – left hand counterclockwise, right hand clockwise. You can move anywhere you like, up or across the body, making the circles larger or smaller as you go.

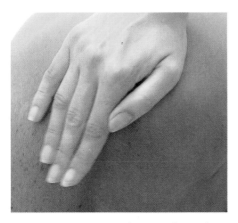

For variation, try making circles with your hands next to one another, both going in the same direction. Or make a circle with one hand, lift it half way through and immediately start another circle from the same place with the other hand, so they are working in unison.

FEATHERING is a series of light, finger-only strokes that works best if you alter the pressure and speed. You can use it so that the hands follow one after the other, move together or work singly. Keep your fingers

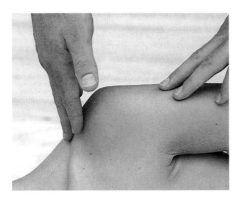

loose and relaxed and do short brushing strokes. It is delicate, soothing, and playful and is doubly enjoyable if you do it in between a series of firmer massage movements. Use it anywhere except very ticklish or sensitive places.

MEDIUM PRESSURE

STRETCHING relieves tension and tightness in muscles and helps extend the body to balance the pull of gravity. Start with your hands together, then pull them apart with a firm, sliding movement, so that they are steadily drawing the muscles and tissue in opposite directions.

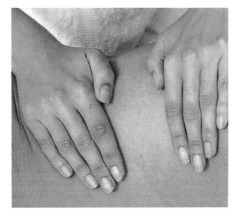

It is particularly good done with hands on either side of the spine, working outwards to the sides, across the width of the shoulder blades, or along the length of the back so one hand finishes near the base of the spine and the other ends between the shoulder blades.

WRINGING is a good movement to use along the sides of the torso or limbs, and over the top of the shoulders, buttocks, or anywhere else where there is looser flesh. Position your hands with fingertips away

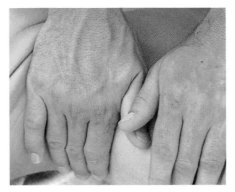

from the direction you are working, and pull one hand towards you, immediately followed by the other. Start with pressure on the fingers and end with it on the palms and repeat the whole movement again and again so it is fluid and flowing.

When you are good at it, you can increase the wringing movement by using your hands alternately so that one hand moves forward as the other hand comes backward.

PRESSING is a gentle but firm downward pressure which you can adapt to use almost anywhere on the body (not directly over the spine). Work with the pads of your thumbs alone, the fingertips, the heel of your hand, or the entire palm – each feels different. You can use both hands for extra pressure. Place in position, gently exert pressure downwards, hold for about ten seconds, then relax. Move across or up the body, repeating as you go. This feels calming and immediately loosens tight areas.

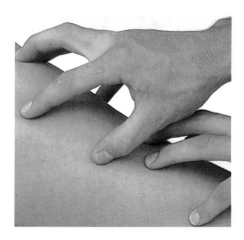

You can use both hands together, but for variation, try one hand following the other, then increase the length of the stroke. Avoid this stroke if you have long fingernails.

DEEP PRESSURE

KNEADING is good for loosening muscles and getting rid of stress. It is just like kneading dough or pastry: gently pinch some flesh between the thumb and closed fingers, then lift and roll it by turning the palms in opposite directions.

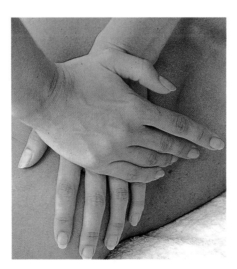

RAKING is particularly soothing after deeper strokes, and can be used just about anywhere. Start by bending your fingers so only the tips are on the skin, then make short firm movements pulling towards you using the rest of the fingers as you go. It is, as its name implies, a raking movement.

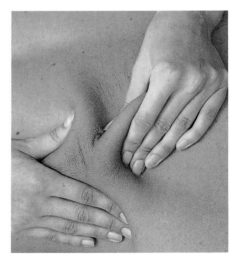

Let go, and without pausing in between, repeat again and again, gradually moving across or up the body. Your hands should maintain constant contact with the skin throughout, so stretch your thumbs wide as you pick up and keep the whole movement rhythmical. It is like a series of constant rocking squeezes that are gentle but firm.

ROTATING may be used on any areas of soft tissue or fleshier parts of the body on top of muscle. It uses only the heels of the hands, which are excellent for applying firm pressure and loosening tension. Start by placing the heel of the hand against the skin, with the palm and fingers raised but relaxed. Then rotate the heel and press

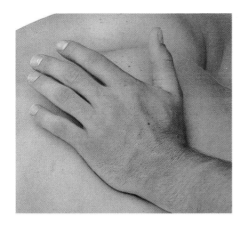

down as you move in small circles, keeping the thumb and fingers loosely splayed upwards and relaxed. With practice, you can vary it by using both hands simultaneously, making circles in opposite directions.

THUMBING uses many movements from other strokes, but all done more deeply and using the thumbs only. The thumbs are very strong, yet small enough to reach into tiny areas, so they are one of the best tools in any massage. Use them to make tiny circles—the right going clockwise and the left going counterclockwise—on either side of the spine for the length of the back. They can be used to do deep, short kneading strokes by pushing one thumb up as the other pulls down. Or push them

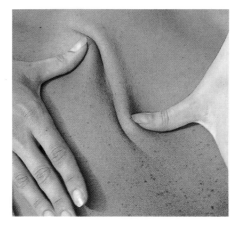

into the skin, move them up an inch, then push them apart in a fanning stroke. Try using thumbs only for stroking, and exert as much pressure as possible. No matter what basic movement you adapt, it will be deeper and more therapeutic if it is done with the thumbs than when you use any other part of the hand.

PLUCKING was said to be Julius Caesar's favourite stroke, when he insisted on his daily massage. Start by pushing gently into soft tissue and picking up a fold of flesh between the fingers and thumb of one hand. Lift gently upwards, then release. As you drop one area of skin you should be picking up another with the other hand, so the whole movement is flowing and continuous. Avoid pinching—it is more like a light, loving squeeze. And gradually move across or up the body as you go.

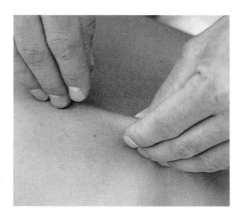

Four step-by-step massages

It's time to get round to enjoying the most sensual, self-indulgent exercise you'll ever do. 'No gain without pain' might be the message of aerobics, but with massage there is no gain without pleasure! And the four basic step-by-step routines described on the following pages are designed to give maximum pleasure in minimum time. Even if you get from start to finish in only 30 minutes, you'll still have worked miracles on your partner.

She'll be relaxed, revitalized, and recharged from your touch. But the basic routines are really designed to be extended for anything up to an hour – if that's what you want. Just increase the repeats by going back to movements you've done before, time and time again. Eventually, you'll throw a few of your own special touches in and throw the book out of the massage room!

These four particular routines have been chosen to pamper the four main areas where touch is most effective: the neck, face and scalp; the back; the feet; the sensual body massage. The programmes contain a mixture of movements that are a comfortable combination of shiatsu, reflexology and Swedish massage, without your having to be an expert in any one of them. (Shiatsu is a Japanese form of massage, using only the fingers on specific, significant points on the body.

partner's body, moulding your hand to his skin and feeling your way. Do more of the movements you – or he – particularly enjoy. Add a few of your own special touches. Experiment and explore. You can only be taught how to start massaging; then, for the rest of your lives, it is up to you to learn how to enjoy it.

Once you feel confident about the massage routines described here, you can experiment with massaging other parts of your partner's body, combining strokes and routines from these massages or making it up yourself. Areas you might think about are the lower back and buttocks, the legs, the hands and the arms (together or separately), and the chest. Rely on what you have already learned and let your imagination – and your hands – lead the way.

Reflexology similarly concentrates on pressing focal points, particularly the nerve endings in the feet. Swedish massage, developed during the nineteenth century, is a system of strong, sweeping strokes, originally designed with muscle therapy in mind.) These techniques have been simplified so they flow naturally from one stroke to the other.

They may be used in any order, alone or together: try the back massage first, followed by the neck, face and scalp, or start your sensual massage by relaxing the feet for 15 minutes before you move on. And if you are short of time, choose between the feet or the back, as they are the quickest ways of relaxing the whole body.

But remember that each of these massage programmes shows you only the basic movements in a natural, flowing order. After the first time, don't follow them exactly. Instead, play with your

You can make any of the massages more therapeutic by adding the right essential oil (see Scents and sensuality, page 72). Some are particularly good for different hair or skin types, some help specific physical problems from headaches to fluid retention, and others alter your emotional mood. So give them a try once you've mastered massage – it will ensure you never get bored or tire of the touch.

But in the meantime, enjoy yourselves!

The neck, face, and scalp massage

Pity the poor head! We think, therefore we inflict headaches. We worry, and every glower, scowl, glare, or subtle frown is held on the face by stress-tensed muscles. We concentrate until our necks feel as though they have been hit by a swing from a sledgehammer. The thin layer of muscle covering the skull tightens like a band and constricts the blood flow to hair follicles – so our crowning glory becomes thin, dull, and lifeless.

All of this, in a day's work; but the tension mounts when it goes on day after day. There is nothing more delicious than massaging it all away. For the face, it is better than any beauty treatment – silicone travels and so do anti-wrinkle potions (usually down the plughole when you wash), and both of them deflate the bank account more than wrinkles. But the touch of your partner's hand instantly relaxes all the tiny subcutaneous muscles of expression; you look better and feel better in one go. Massaging the scalp has the added benefit of increasing natural oil secretions so the hair grows better: but even the tiny amount of oil you rub in will leave it healthier and glossier than any bottle of conditioner. For the neck and shoulders, massage not only gets rid of the feeling of tension (stiffness, aching and dull pain), but it also removes the signs of it (stooping, hunching, and a curved chest).

Throughout this massage your partner should lie on her back, with cushions for comfort where needed. The head should be slightly raised so the neck and shoulders relax (a telephone directory will do perfectly). And you should kneel behind her head while you work. While massaging her face, you might prefer to rest her head on a cushion between your crossed legs – this makes it even more intimate and relaxing. And as facial skin is so delicate, use enough oil to avoid dragging or pulling too much. Be gentle; it needs a light, sensual touch throughout to be totally relaxing.

● With oil on your hands, slide them under your partner's back so they rest on either side of the spine, and draw them steadily up the neck to stretch out the muscles (stroking movement). Repeat, using more oil if needed. Place one hand over each

1. Using your fingertips only, sweep from the shoulders up the neck in a raking movement.
2. Place one hand, with fingers and thumb extended, under her head where the neck meets the skull bone, and squeeze and lift gently as you push down on her forehead with the palm of the hand.

1

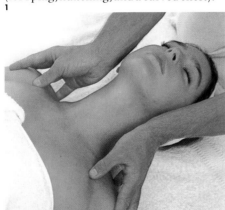

2

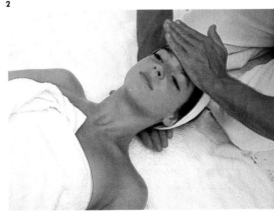

3

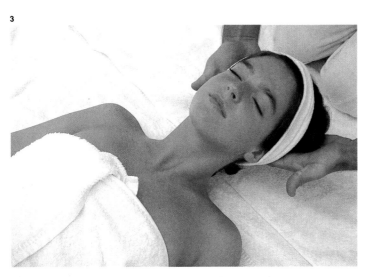

**3. Lift and support
her head with both
hands, then gently
rotate in circles
moving clockwise to
the right and
counterclockwise to
the left.
4. Work along the
shoulder muscles
from the neck to the
arms, using a
wringing movement.
5. Run your fingers
through her hair and
tug it gently, pulling
close to the roots.**

shoulder and using your fingertips only (raking movement) gently sweep them in towards the neck and up to the sides of the ears (1). Repeat.

● Place one hand flat on the forehead and position the thumb and index finger of the other hand under the head, where the top of the neck meets the skull (2). Push gently down on the forehead as you squeeze and lift with the other hand supporting the back of the head (pressing movement). Hold for a count of five, then repeat. This relaxes the muscles and instantly releases tension. With your hands in the same position, slowly turn the head from side to side, supporting it throughout. Repeat.

● With both hands supporting the back of the neck where it meets the skull (as done with one hand, before), gently lift and

rotate the head, making slow figure eight movements – clockwise circles to the right side as half your figure eight, then loop up and over counterclockwise to the left side (3). These should be slow, and raise the head only a couple of inches.

● Slip your fingers with palms upwards on either side of the neck, and, working along the top of the shoulder muscles from the nape of the neck out to each arm, pull your partner's skin up towards you (wringing movement) (4). Repeat both sides of each shoulder and change to a thumbing or kneading movement as you go. Finish by holding the thumbs where the shoulder muscle meets the outer collar bone and push down firmly for a count of ten.

● Using the pads of your fingertips only, loosen your partner's scalp by rubbing as if

5

shampooing her hair. Start at the front and move up to the crown and down to the nape of the neck. Try to push down (pressing movement) with the finger pads and make the scalp itself rotate in small circles to release the tension in the underlying muscles. Then run your fingers through the hair before repeating again all over. Then take sections of hair between your fingers and thumb and tug repeatedly and firmly (5). It won't hurt if you pick it up as close to the roots as possible. Finally, squeeze the head between the hands, pushing from side to side and back to front, and end up by pushing down into the crown with the finger pads only, holding for a count of ten.

4

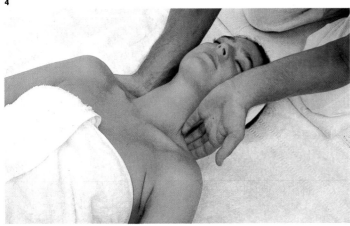

6

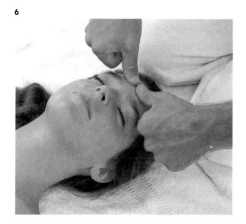

● Using two fingertips or your thumbs, rub and rotate the skin over your partner's temples (circling movement). Repeat and finish by pressing and holding for a count of ten. Using thumbs only, push down for a count of four (pressing movement) between the eyebrows and continue to press every half inch as you work in a line up towards the hair (6). Start another row of thumb presses one inch out on either side and repeat in lines moving upward and outward until the last repeat works along the top of the eyebrows and finishes at the outer eye corner, near the temples. Finally, sweep the forehead upwards, alternating the palms of your hands (stroking movement) in a gentle, flowing motion.

● Gently oil the whole face by sweeping your hands (stroking movement) from the chest up the neck to the chin; take one hand out along either side of the jawbone, then up past the ears, across the cheeks to the

7

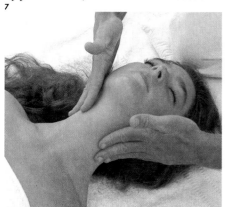

nose, and down again (7). Repeat a lot, varying the speed and movements (from stroking to gentle feathering). Using two fingers together then lightly pulling apart (stretching movement), work the length of the nose, with one finger ending at the bridge and the other at the tip, and then across the forehead, centre to outer sides. Repeat all this step as often as you wish, exploring different parts of the face as you go.

● Using your fingertips only, start at the bridge of the nose and stroke out along the eyebrows, round the temples, and back under the eyes to the nose in a circle (8). Repeat with hands working simultaneously or alternately. Using both index finger pads, push down as lightly as possible on the inner eyes (over tear ducts), then move down along the cheekbones to the outer eye corners (pressing movement), and back up the brows to the inner eyes. Finish by resting your fingers gently across the eyes with the softest pressure and pause for a count of five.

Repeat any of the different steps of the massage or the entire procedure again as often as you wish, but always end with this final step.

8

6. Press your thumbs down on her forehead, every half inch from her brows up to the hairline.
7. Gently oil the face with slow stroking movements starting from the chest up to the neck, the chin, across the jaw, and sweeping back around the entire face.
8. Using your fingertips only, make slow, soft circles from between the brows right around the eyes, several times.

The back massage

The back is undoubtedly the easiest place to give a really good rub. It is the biggest single part of the body, so there is a lot of room to play and experiment and make huge sweeping gestures – for which it is eternally grateful. It has more muscles than any other area and a jigsaw puzzle of 26 interlocking bones called the spine. Together, they carry the weight of the rest of our bodies, from holding the head up to balancing our floppy limbs as we move about.

1. Spread the oil with light sweeping strokes up the back to feel tense muscles before starting.

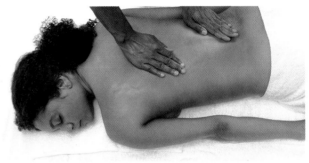

2. Use cross stretching to relax muscles, by sliding hands across the torso, from hip to opposite shoulder.

They carry a huge load of tension as well, especially as the back upholsters the sensitive spinal cord, which is the largest bundle of nerve fibres outside the brain. That's what gets an urgent message from your toe to your head in the same time it takes to make a telephone connection between London and New York.

The back also has to balance the

3

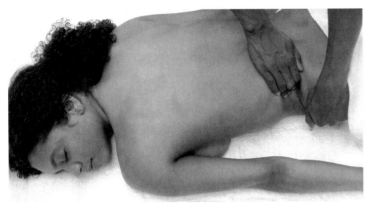

**3. Working along the sides of the body, use a wringing movement to pull skin up towards the middle of the torso.
4. Using your thumbs only, make small circles from the waist to the neck on either side of the spinal column.**

4

delights of life, like carrying a heavy load, wearing high heels or working over a word processor. All of them add to its burden and end up making it tight, tense, and aching. But a simple back massage goes beyond just relaxing the back muscles – it affects the entire body, thanks to all the nerve fibres sited there. It sends soothing waves of pleasure straight to the brain. It pushes sluggish lymph and blood back to be cleansed and wakes up the whole circulation system.

The main areas where tension builds up are the lower back on either side of the waist, and the upper back above the shoulders – and this is where the deep massage strokes work wonders. But first, it is important to relax the entire network of support muscles with lots of sweeping light and medium pressure strokes. Keep any skin you're not working on covered with a towel. Obviously, your partner has to lie face down, but let her position her arms in the most natural way.

● Start making light sweeps up the entire back (stroking movement) to spread the oil and warm the muscles (1). Feel the body contours as you go and try to pinpoint tight muscles or lumpy, tense areas. Gradually increase the pressure of upward strokes, but keep downward ones light. Eventually, increase the speed and change the rhythm. Then spread the hands out across the shoulders on the upward strokes. Repeat, then include some variations of fanning by ending the downward stroke with a figure eight across the waist and round the buttocks.
● Without pausing, begin some stretching movements. First slide your hands the length of the back so one pulls from the base of the spine and the other from between the shoulders. Repeat, then stretch with one hand on either side of the spine moving simultaneously out to the sides, from the bottom to top of the back. Try some cross stretching, so one hand ends over the hip and the other on the opposite shoulder blade (2). Each movement should be one, long, firm stroke to stretch muscles and skin.
● With your hands under your partner's hip, pull flesh up and toward the centre of the torso (wringing movement), working all the way up the side of her body, across the shoulders and down the other side (3). Then try it just across the waist, bringing both hands simultaneously toward the middle of the back before crossing them and continuing with hands pulling up again from opposite sides in one flowing movement. Repeat.

● With your hands palm down on either side of the waist, start rotating up the back to the shoulders (circling movement). Make larger circles around the whole shoulder blade at the top. Repeat, using your thumbs only (4) to make small, deeper circles from bottom to top (thumbing movement). Finish by placing thumbs about two inches out from either

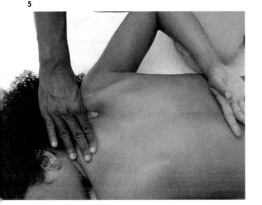

side of the spine and pushing down for a count of four, then repeating a few inches higher (pressing movement).

● Bend your partner's arm and lift it up, placing her hand on the middle of her back and resting her elbow on your leg – this makes the shoulder blade relax and jut out so you can reach the underlying muscle. Using your thumbs only, work under and around the projecting shoulder blade with circling or kneading strokes (5). Release the arm and continue kneading the muscles along the top of the shoulder. Swap sides and repeat again.

● Using both hands, spend some time feeling every contour of your partner's back, using raking, kneading, deep stroking, and rotating movements. Work first on the buttocks and lower back, with a towel over the shoulders to keep them warm, then swap and concentrate on the middle back and shoulders. Go over the entire back, loosely picking up and dropping any fleshy areas (6). Finish with long, slow alternate strokes the length of the back, so one hand is moving up as the other is moving down.

● Use both hands, heels only, followed

next time by the whole hand, and do a series of pressing movements. Start on each buttock (7), then the hips, and gradually move up the back to the top of the armpits. Then place one hand over each shoulder above the arms and pull down toward the feet. Finally, place one hand on top of the other and push gently down over the small of the back. Hold each press for a count of ten and raise your

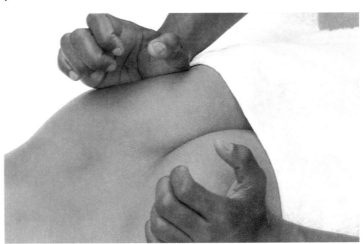

hands afterwards in a smooth, very tactile movement.

● Run your index and third finger down either side of the spine from the neck to the base of the spine (8). Keep a gentle but even pressure throughout and move as slowly as possible. Repeat, then, to end the massage, use light brushing strokes (feathering movement) all over the back in an upward and downward motion.

5. Bend her arm so her hand rests on her back.
6. Pluck loose skin all over.
7. Do a series of presses.
8. Run two fingers down either side of the spine.

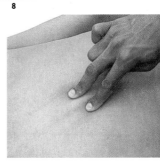

The foot massage About 200,000 years ago *Homo erectus* took his first upright steps using the typical striding gait that characterizes modern man. Since then we've never looked back, or downwards much either. We tend to ignore what lies below the ankles. Feet are expected to be bound and gagged in shoes all day and then dance the light fantastic all night. We step on things, kick things, climb, trip, and stumble through our lives, and then expect to be able to run to catch a bus.

When we walk a mile, we stride about 900 times and at each step the foot carries twice our body weight. If you weigh 150 pounds, that means they cope with about 120 tons of force per mile.

Most of us don't even like our feet and think they are ugly and lumpy and callused, as if it was their fault, and not ours. The physical abuse doesn't just make them look less than beautiful. It affects how we feel. Tired feet drag on the whole body, so we shuffle around in a bad mood rather than trotting with a smile and a skip. And tension from other worries ends up there, because the feet are richly supplied with nerve endings from all over the body. There are 72,000 in each foot, twined around almost a quarter of all the bones we own (28 from toe to heel), all held in place by an intricate web of 38 muscles. This is why the feet are so sensitive yet capable of carrying your weight on the arch and absorbing the shock of impact on the sole.

A good foot massage lightens your step and rubs away the tension of a hard day's work. It also keeps feet healthy and flexible. And it is strangely intimate and deeply sensual. Your partner should lie face down so you can kneel and cushion her foot on your bent legs. Start with only a little oil, or your fingers will slide about and feel ticklish. Work gently on the top of the foot because the skin is thin here and there are a lot of tiny bones. Under the toes and the sole you need a firmer touch, although the arch can also be sensitive. And don't be afraid to pick them up and play with them. The feet are as receptive to sensual strokes as many of the body's more glamorous zones.

● Pick up one of your partner's feet and, resting it on your thigh, vigorously rub the

1. Vigorously rub her heel between the palms of your hands to spread the oil, and warm and relax the entire foot.
2. Resting her foot flat along your leg, knead under the arch of the foot, using your thumbs only, and finish up with long, sweeping thumb strokes.

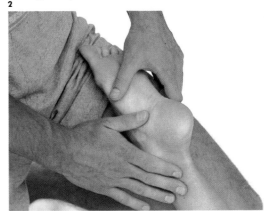

3

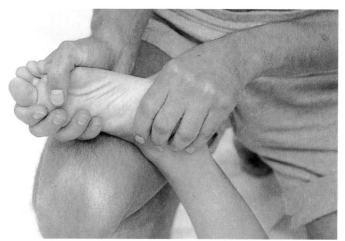

3. Squeeze and twist the foot, using a wringing movement.

4. Supporting the foot by the heel and toes, flex it gently by pointing the toes slowly upwards and then downwards.

5. Play with her toes, by pulling each one gently between your thumb and index finger, before twisting them with a corkscrew movement.

heel with your oiled palms, one hand moving forwards while the other moves backwards (1). Continue until the foot is warm – this stimulates the circulation and relaxes the whole foot. Using more oil, sweep the foot (stroking movement) from the ankle to the toes, with one hand working along the top and the other along the sole. Repeat.

● Rest the top of your partner's foot flat along your leg. Using only your thumbs, push down firmly on the heel and count to four (pressing movement) then repeat every half inch in a line up to the toes. Then starting with your thumbs on the ball of the foot, work back towards the heel making small, deep circular movements along and across the foot. Finally, knead with your thumbs under the arch of the

foot and finish off with long thumb sweeps the length of the arch (2).

● Move to the side so your partner's foot rests across one of your legs. Squeeze and twist the foot (wringing movement) by holding one hand around the heel and the other around the toes and twisting in opposite directions (3). Do the same movement with your hands around only the arch of the foot. Repeat.

● Hold your partner's foot upright, the leg bent at the knee, with one hand around the heel and the other over the toes. Flex the foot by pushing the toes down to the floor (4) and up to the ceiling. Then swing the

5

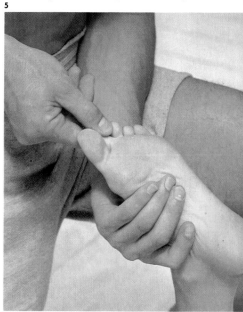

foot from side to side, still supporting the heel and pushing from the toes. Finally, in the same position, rotate the foot by making circles in the air with the toes. Repeat.

● With your partner's leg still bent at the knee, hold her foot upright with one hand gripped round the arch. With the other hand, gently pull each toe in turn with your index finger and thumb (5). Then starting with the big toe, twist from side to side like a corkscrew, letting your thumb and finger slide off the end. Repeat on each toe. Then lace your bent fingers between the toes and work them backwards and

4

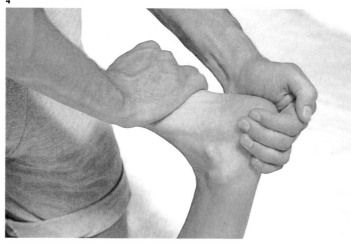

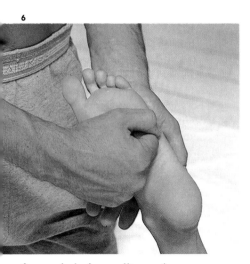

6

forwards, before pulling up by straightening your fingers and pushing the toes into the palm of your hand. Repeat.

● With the foot lying flat on the floor, place your thumbs on the sole, your palms around the sides and your fingers on the top of the foot. Work the bones deep within the foot by pressing out and down with the thumbs and heel of each hand, from one end of the foot to the other. Then rotate the bones by pulling one hand up (toward you) while the other pushes down (away from you). Repeat, pushing and pulling in opposite directions. Then gently knead the whole foot simultaneously, using your fingers on the top as your thumbs work on the sole. Finally hold the top of the foot with the palm of one hand, make the other into a fist and press into the

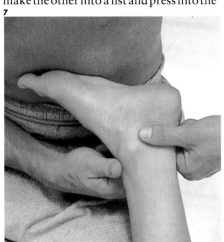

7

ball and arch of the foot in a back and forward kneading movement, supporting as you push down into the other hand (6).

● Grip the ankle with the thumb and fingers of one hand, encircling it and squeezing deeply before releasing. Repeat using both hands and twist them in opposite directions to wring the loose skin around the ankle. Then using your thumbs only, make small, light circles all around the ankle, from the middle out to the sides, down around the bone, and up the back of the heel (7). Repeat.

● Finally, stroke the entire foot, pulling one hand from the ankle along the top and the other hand from the heel along the sole (8). End by pulling the toes upward between the palms in a firm, flowing movement. Repeat several times, then begin the massage from step 1 on your partner's other foot.

8

6. Hold the top of the foot with one hand and using your fist, press and knead into the arch of the foot.
7. Using your thumbs only, make small, light circles right around the ankle bone.
8. Sandwich her foot between the palms of your hands and sweep from the ankle to the toes.

The sensual body massage A complete body massage not only wipes away tension but builds a greater feeling of intimacy between you and your partner. It is a potent form of touch, using as much skin on skin as possible. We rarely allow ourselves 30 minutes of pure sensory – rather than sexual – pleasure, but if we did more often, we would be more in touch with our partner's desires. By not emphasizing the obviously erotic, you can create some delicious sensations all over the body.

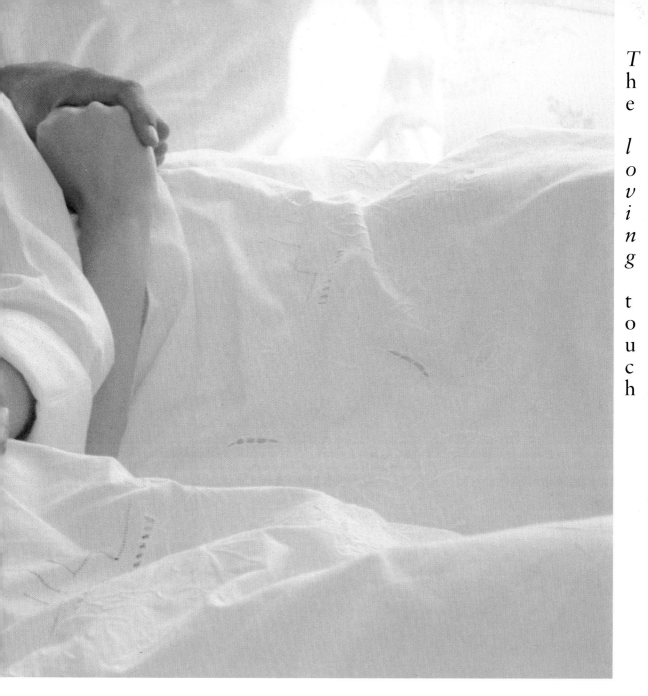

1. Make slow sweeps up the back, then bend forward using your body weight to stretch muscles.

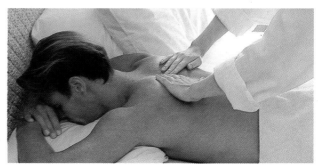

2. Use both hands to make slow, sensual circles around his shoulders, keeping your bodies close.

The main thing to remember during a sensual massage is to take your time and use long, unhurried soothing strokes. The slower you go, the stronger the anticipation of what happens next. And by using your whole body to give pleasure, you will develop a more rewarding kind of touch than you thought possible. Use your wrists and arms as well as your hands to make body contact as you do the massage movements. And feel free to nuzzle or kiss your partner's body if it seems natural. But remember, this type of massage is not about erogenous zones, but about sensory awareness and exploring bodies. After years together, you can discover that knees are as pleasurable as nipples.

● With your partner lying face down, start applying oil with a firm, slow full body stroke. Place your palms on the soles of his feet and push upwards over the heels, running one hand curved across each calf to the back of the knees. Continue up the thighs, and rest your hands on the buttocks as you move up to kneel on either side. Continue the sweep up the back, out across the shoulders and down each arm until you are pulling his fingers downward. Repeat.
● Starting from the lower back, make long, slow sweeps up to the shoulders, leaning forward and pressing your chest to his back as you pull your hands down, so your body weight helps stretch the muscles (1). Repeat. Do the same

movement, but spread your hands across the shoulders at the top of the stroke so your hands move back down the sides of the torso and draw firmly inwards at the waist. Repeat, then do the same stroke with a figure eight movement from the waist down around the buttocks and back up to the hips. Repeat.
● Using the heels of your hands, followed by the palms, make slow, strong circles over the buttocks first simultaneously, then alternately. Finish by pushing the heels of your hands into the hollows on each buttock for a count of ten. Then use the whole hand to make circles from the hips round and up to the waist, keeping them slow and sensual. Do the same from the outer arms, along the neck and around

4

the shoulders, leaning low over your partner's back (2). Do a series of finger only strokes (feathering movement) from the buttocks up to the neck, taking your time and feeling every contour of the back as you go. Finally, using the length of your arm from elbow to wrist, held across his back, make upward sweeping strokes.
● Cover the back with towels and move down to your partner's feet. Press the palms of your hands down into the soles of the feet and sweep upwards to the knee. Repeat. Encircling the ankles with your outstretched thumbs and fingers, push firmly up to the knees several times. Then place your palms flat together mid-thigh and pull your hands apart until one rests under the buttock crease and the other above the knee (stretching movement).

To make the massage sensual and intimate take your time and throw in some of your own special touches.
3. Use a wringing movement on inner and outer legs.
4. Make long, slow, sweeping strokes from the hips up to his chest and out, ending by pushing down into the hollow at the top of the arms.
3

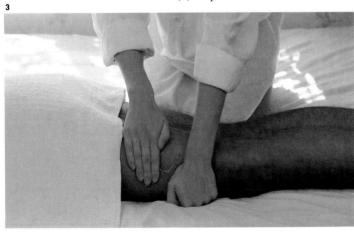

5

**5. With one hand on top of the other, make slow, soft circles, over the abdomen in a clockwise direction.
6. Pay extra attention to the knees, by lifting and rolling the loose skin upwards, in a light, gentle plucking movement.**

Hold for a count of five, then repeat. Finally, stroke the inner and outer legs from ankle to thigh, using your fingertips – first with a wringing movement (3), then with an upwards feathering movement.

● With your partner lying face up, apply oil by repeating the full body stroke. Then kneel on either side of his thighs. Starting from the hips, make long, slow sweeps up to the middle of the chest and across, ending by pushing down into the natural hollow where the top of the arms meet the collarbones (4). Hold for a count of five, then bend over and lower your chest as you pull back down the sides of the body, drawing your hands in across the waist.

● Using the palms of your hands, make slow circles from under the buttocks in to the waist, over the hips and down to the top of the thighs. Then place your palms on either hip and gently press out and down, holding for a count of five, and repeat as you move your hand down either side of the loins. With one hand on top of the other, make soft, slow circles over the abdomen in a clockwise direction (5). Then stroke the whole torso upwards, starting from the tummy and moving up to the neck. Finish by pushing down with flat hands held over the outer shoulders, the biceps, the elbow crease, the wrist and the palms, for a count of five, before holding and pulling the fingers.

6

● Cover the upper body with towels and move down to your partner's feet. Repeat all of step 4, but pay extra attention to the knees. Stroke them on either side and make circles with your fingers around the kneecaps. Then starting below each knee, lift and roll the loose skin, working upwards (plucking movement) (6).

● Finish with a full body press. Remove all towels and lie on top of your partner, stretched out comfortably from head to toe. Relax totally and enjoy the warmth of one another's skin on skin. Breathe slowly and keep your heads close together on the pillow. After a few minutes, lie side by side with your arms wrapped around one another and give in to gravity so your bodies feel heavy. Touch each other as much as possible and enjoy the feeling of peace and quiet.

Scents *and* sensuality were even more important than touch for ensuring survival of the human race. Our primeval ancestors relied on smell to find food, detect enemies, recognize mates, and track down the camp fires of nearby tribes. Today, we know food is at the nearest supermarket, our enemies wear deodorant, our lovers smell of perfume, and our friends' homes are found from street names printed on maps. Consequently, we rely on our sense of smell as little as humanly possible.

Despite the fact that we breathe more than 23,000 times each day and shift 500 cubic feet of air through the nose, modern man only bothers to notice particularly good or bad smells – everything in between isn't registered in the conscious mind. But that doesn't mean these aromas have no effect. When we are hungry, the smell of food immediately triggers digestive juices and saliva. When we are tense and irritable, the smell of flowers in full bloom changes our mood. When we're tired, the smell of coffee brewing can energize us as much as the taste.

Scientists know very little about smell; touch, taste, hearing, and sight are simple by comparison. It is the one sense that leads directly from the outside world to the brain. The olfactory receptors are the only nerves in the human body exposed to air, and there are five to ten million of them in each nostril, in two patches the size of a postage stamp. They do know that the left nostril takes an aroma message to the left (or logical) side of the human brain, and that the right nostril delivers to the right (or intuitive) side. So the smell is named on the left and logged or described on the right. It is the quickest of our five senses – we know within 0.5 of a second whether there is an apple or an old sock under our nose, yet it takes us three times longer to recognize the sound of someone knocking on the front door. But exactly how we decipher and recognize one scent out of the 10,000 or more we are capable of smelling is still a mystery.

This is because our sense of smell still occupies the same portion of the brain that it did from the very beginning of the human race. The fact that our lifestyle has evolved so that smell is no longer vital for survival or procreation is irrelevant physiologically. Everything we sniff is registered in the limbic area – the 'old' brain. And in response to our needs over the centuries, this area of the brain has expanded its functions beyond that of a smell organ, to include emotions, sexual behaviour, artistic abilities, creativity, cognitive thought, memory, hunger, thirst, and body temperature. This now means that human perception of smell is deeply linked to these other functions of the limbic centre of the brain.

When we smell chalk we may feel the childish panic we had in the schoolroom; a particular perfume puts us back in our grandmother's lap; a whiff of antiseptic invokes the fear of being in hospital; and the smell of seaweed or suntan oil instantly puts us in the holiday mood. Every single smell we've ever encountered is part of an emotion or memory that paints the overall picture of exactly what the smell is to us. Furthermore, this picture is unique because, with the exception of identical twins, no two people perceive the same smell in the same way. This is why we can smell cheese and may think 'Yuk, strong, tangy Roquefort', or 'Yum, mild, tasty cheddar', depending on previous experience. When a mouse smells cheese it can't get beyond 'Food' – otherwise it might think 'Mousetrap?' and learn to be a bit more discerning.

However, this is no reason to feel superior to the mouse. He, along with most other animals in the world, uses his sense of smell on a level that mankind has forgotten. A salmon can recognize the scent of the stream where it hatched from hundreds of miles across the ocean and return to the same place to spawn. A camel can smell an oasis 50 miles across the desert. And a male moth can sniff out a prospective mate as she flutters unknowlingly round a garden on the opposite side of Los Angeles, despite the smog that stretches between them. Modern man's sense of smell once had similar powers, but they have declined through lack of use: for instance, only 250 years ago American Indians sniffed the ground to follow the minute traces of smell left by another human being, and in Africa tribesmen still hunt animals by following their noses. Research proves that, even today, our sense of smell is most acute when we are hungry – but these days, it will lead us into a restaurant rather than down to the river to catch supper.

Although we still give off body scents, or pheromones – the natural secretions that a moth uses to find a mate or dogs use to follow a fox during the hunt – we no longer bother to smell them. In fact, we spend most of our lives disguising them with deodorant, aftershave, talcum powder, or perfume, to the extent that we only believe our hair is clean if it smells clean (even though it is the detergent, not the fragrance in shampoo that actually removes the dirt). Scientists believe that we still respond unconsciously to our pheromones and that they influence sexual attraction and bonding between partners. This has been proved in a recent study in West Germany, where 75 couples wore cotton T-shirts for a week without using any toiletries. Then, they were blindfolded and asked to sniff out their partner's shirt from its smellprint – and most of them succeeded with astounding accuracy.

It is the nose that gives us 80 percent of all the information about what we eat. Our tongue provides the other 20 percent – sweet, sour, salty, and bitter are all there is to taste. This is why we lose our appetites when we have a heavy cold. Without a keen sense of smell, a sliver of onion tastes the same as a slice of apple.

Winning by a nose

On a daily basis, we now use our sense of smell mainly for pleasure, to differentiate between things we like or dislike. It is the nose that tells us what we feel about everything we encounter, from a traffic jam to a bunch of freesias, from rotting fish to a new brand of perfume. Some of these likes and dislikes are inherent: research has shown that even newborn babies screw up their little noses at some smells and gurgle happily at others. But most of our preferences are learned through experience, and become tied up with emotion, memory, and all the other functions of the limbic system. So in a world where we ignore what is under our noses and use only a fraction of its full potential, we are missing out on one of the greatest pleasures of smell – and that is its therapeutic effect.

Without realizing, we use smell to alter our moods: when we take flowers to a sick person, when we smear eucalyptus oil on our chests to clear a head cold, or when we buy a new perfume as a cheer-up treat. These are obvious examples, but, on a deeper level of consciousness, we only need walk past newly mown grass to feel instantly lightfooted and less pressured. We register smell more keenly as the day goes by and our noses wake up. We lose our sense of smell as we age: at 20, we notice 82 percent of aromas, by 80, this level has dropped to 28 percent – mainly due to lack of practice. Women are most sensitive to smell during the first half of their menstrual cycle, peaking at ovulation when they are most fertile. For some reason, men can smell tar and coffee better than women. And in summer, both sexes notice an increased aroma impact due to the warmer weather.

But this is pretty basic stuff compared to what researchers now know about the mind-body effects of smell. They have discovered that the right smell can put us in the right mood, even though they are no closer to finding out how or why it does. So their main priority over the next decade is to link behaviour with fragrance to create an accurate sniff-and-tell list – and the race is on worldwide to see who can do it first.

Already in the United States, the Fragrance Foundation, an organization dedicated to researching the sense of smell, has awarded grants to dozens of universities whose clinical psychologists are studying the effects of smell and stress, work performance, sleep, and social relationships. In Great Britain, the Olfaction Research Group at Warwick University has a team of biochemists turning the latest high-tech equipment onto the oldest sense: there is a computer nose, with 400 individual scent receptors connected to a microchip. For the first time, scientists can see what happens

when we inhale an aroma; they are using machines to measure any changes in brain-wave activity due to smell. And dozens of clinical trials are underway, including the use of fragrance to treat seriously disturbed patients in mental hospitals. In Japan, the Shimizu Construction Company has developed a patented computer system for delivering smells to large buildings through the air conditioning. The company is working in conjunction with the Takasago Corporation, Japan's largest fragrance manufacturer, to isolate the right smells to use. Between them they have already proved that lemon can energize office workers first thing in the morning, jasmine can soothe weary hotel guests, lavender can help lessen mental fatigue at business meetings, peppermint can activate the circulatory system at the gym, and cinnamon piped into reception areas can

induce calmness. They are continuing their studies using systems in a tourist centre and a home for the elderly.

Ironically, all this research into the future of smell has been triggered by ancient knowledge. For thousands of years humans have used fragrant, natural extracts from herbs, flowers, fruits, barks, and resins to cure and cosset one another. It is a technique that has pottered along using only trial and error to perfect and

refine its therapeutic effects. But as researchers use modern techniques to verify how individual smells alter our moods, their scientific proof confirms what we have always known empirically. And this ancient knowledge is all ready and waiting for you to enjoy. It is called aromatherapy, and it is the simplest and most pleasurable way of stimulating the nose, the mind, and the body simultaneously.

Our sense of smell stimulates the nose, the mind, and the body, by triggering memories, changing moods, arousing emotions, and telling us if we like or dislike everything we encounter.

Aromatherapy: the sensual science

Aromatherapy is a treatment using powerful substances called essential oils. It combines two equally important areas: 'aroma' comes from the natural smell of the plant, and this gives pleasure, alters moods and affects the mind in as many different ways as there are different smells; and 'therapy' comes from the natural curative and medicinal properties of the plants which include thousands of remedies.

Nobody really knows what essential oils are. It is known how to extract and use them, and that when we inhale their vapours or rub them on our skin they have astounding effects on our mental and physical well-being. Exactly what they do for a plant is still a mystery.

In the laboratory they break down into terpenes, esters, aldehydes, phenols, alcohols, ketones, and hundreds of other ingredients that are so small they defy the most powerful microscope. This is why they manage to beat our most impenetrable defence – human skin. When we jump into a bath we don't drown and if we rubbed in a shot of gin we wouldn't get drunk, but when essential oils are applied anywhere on our bodies, they travel through our fatty tissue to the interstitial fluid round body cells, and into the blood, lymph, and organs, before being naturally excreted. Individual essential oils seem to gravitate to different parts of the body. For instance lavender and ylang ylang, which both have a soothing or calming effect, seem to have an affinity with the nervous system within four hours of application. Although scientific tests prove that many essential oils gravitate to many different areas of the body, scientists are light years away from understanding what leads them or holds them there.

But knowing how essential oils work is less important than knowing that they do. While researchers keep researching, they are merely putting the official scientific stamp of approval to an instinctive therapy that dates back thousands of years to the original witch doctor. The trial by error started when man first came to this Earth and set about learning which plants and fruits were beneficial and which were fatal. This knowledge was passed on verbally until life got beyond mere survival and became pleasurable. The Egyptian healers wrote down all they knew on papyrus and left us hard proof of how clever they were – one example being Tutankhamen, who was wrapped with myrrh and cedarwood oil and didn't look bad for his age 3,300 years later, when his tomb was discovered in 1922. Nero, who loved scents almost as much as orgies, had rosewater sprayed from silver pipes in his dining room walls to help his guests banish their hangovers and put them in the mood for post-prandial entertainments. In India sandalwood ruled, in Tibet musk, in China camphor, and Arabians valued myrrh.

By the sixteenth century, European men and women used liberal applications of naturally fragrant waters in lieu of soap and water for personal hygiene. By the time the Great Plague hit London in 1665, the power of plants ruled supreme, as recorded in a jingle that is still a popular nursery rhyme: 'Ring-a-ring o' roses (thought to be the red circles that appeared on the body as the first sign of the disease), a pocket full of posies (pine, cypress, lavender and cedar, carried to ward off the

We take flowers to cheer a sick friend, yet a single drop of the essential oil of rose captures the sweet, sensual aroma of an entire garden of roses in full bloom.

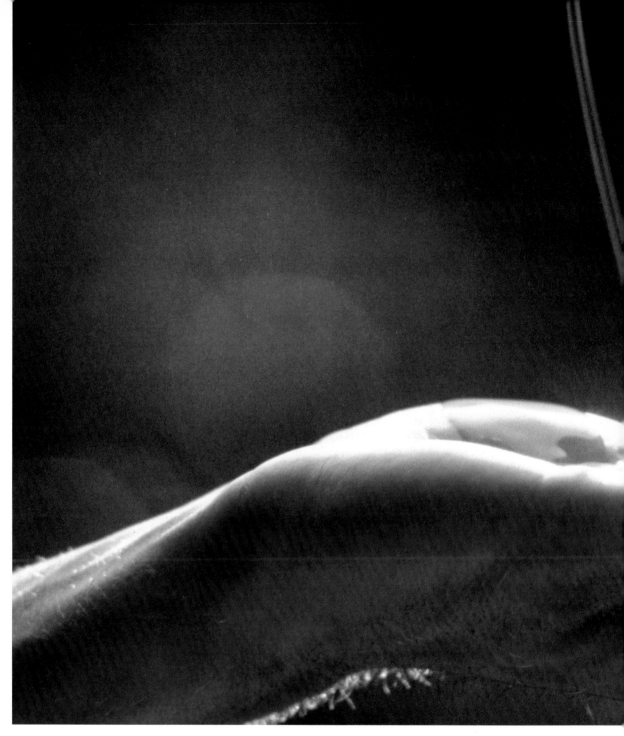

Plague), A-tishoo! A-tishoo! (the second stage of the disease), we all fall down' (or drop dead, presumably). Despite the whimsy of the nursery rhyme, it is now known that pine, cypress, lavender, and cedar – which were burned in the streets and sickrooms as well as being carried – are powerful antiseptics.

Herbalists continued to dispense the only form of medicine – ointments, oils, infusions, poultices, and incenses all made from plants – until the late nineteenth century. From the Iroquois Indians in North America, who drank infusions of spruce tree to prevent scurvy (spruce is now known to be rich in vitamin C), to the Maoris in New Zealand, who used manuka to treat dysentery, burns, and wounds (the plant is now called tea-tree and its essential oil has proved to be 12 times stronger than carbolic acid, the commonest antiseptic of recent times),

herbal treatments were used worldwide. But the advance of modern medicine changed our approach to healing to the extent that anything primitive came second to anything scientific. Instead of drinking a cup of peppermint tea to cure indigestion, we soon learned to swallow an antacid tablet, which contains, among other things, a mint extract. Although the wrappings of contemporary processing disguise it convincingly, essential oils are

still used today: mainly as food flavourings (what would marmalade be without lemon and lime, or chewing gum without spearmint?), to make perfumes (think of Chanel No 5 minus the hawthorn, jonquil, rose, and jasmine), and in medicines (take away the eucalyptus and Vicks VapoRub would never have left North Carolina, where pharmacist Lunsford Richardson first mixed it over 75 years ago).

Essential oils are so potent that they need to be diluted before being applied to the skin: if you mix a small amount you won't tire of the aroma, and can try a different combination with every massage.

Although essential oils are still potent on this basic level, their true powers are capable of far more when used properly. And despite the knowledge gleaned over 5,000 years, the word 'aromatherapy' has been heard only in the last 50. The term was coined by a French chemist named Réné-Maurice Gattefossé, who burned his hand in his laboratory and plunged it into a jar of lavender oil – thereby gaining first hand experience of its power to heal burns. He spent the rest of his life studying essential oils and wrote many papers about his work on *aromathérapie*. After that, the name, and his amazing discoveries, caught on. They were practised by a famous French physician, Dr. Jean Valnet, who wrote a book entitled *Aromathérapie* in 1964, which is still the aromatherapists' bible. It was the French biochemist Marguerite Maury, an ardent teacher of aromatherapy until her death in 1964, who developed the unique method of applying essential oils with massage that is used worldwide today. It is this simple idea of pampering with both touch and smell in one go that makes modern aromatherapy so powerful and such a delight.

Down to the essentials

There are about 800 natural aromatic plants used in perfumery, and of these, a quarter are known to have specific therapeutic value. Those who specialize in aromatherapy, rely on a vital list of around 30 essential oils for all their treatments – and these are now readily available from manufacturers and retailers worldwide (see page 142 for a list of aromatherapy associations and useful addresses).

The essential oils themselves are held in tiny sacs found in the leaves, petals, berries, fruits, stems, and barks of plants. And just like wines, they have good and bad years. The quality and purity of oils depends on the climate, the moment of harvest, and the method of extraction. In

The leaves, petals, berries, fruits, stems, and barks of plants need to be harvested at the right moment to extract the purest, highest quality essential oil.

the world of perfumery, the person who creates the scent is called a 'nose' and the 20 Great Noses working in the industry today are so skilled that they can tell the place and the year a particular oil was produced just by sniffing it. In the South of France, white jasmine flowers are picked at dawn, before they are a day old, and 8 million blooms yield a single kilogram of oil, while roses are harvested mid-May, with 2,000kg of petals plucked to provide an ounce of oil. This is why these are the most expensive to buy.

Pepper oil comes from the unripe berries, ylang-ylang blooms in Madagascar, clove can be extracted only after the buds are picked and dried, and the sandalwood tree has to be 30 years old and grow to 30 feet tall in India before it even produces any oil. Some plants contain several oils: petitgrain oil comes from the leaves, neroli from the blossom, and orange oil from the fruit rind of the same citrus tree. And they appear in the most surprising variety of hues: patchouli is burgundy, violet is dark green, camomile blue, and others range from vivid yellow to deep gold.

Extracting these magical substances from the tiny sacs where they form is a complicated and sophisticated process. Some are distilled so that they evaporate in steam and are then separated from the water once they've cooled. Others need to be pressed on a base of solidified fat until, months later, it is saturated with the essential oil, which is then removed with alcohol. Gums and resins are dissolved in solvents, bark is pulverized, powdered, and then separated, and fruit rinds are squeezed over sponges to collect the precious droplets of liquid. And since all essential oils are not oily at all, what you are left with is a light, highly volatile liquid that must be carefully stored in dark glass containers – otherwise all that hard work is in vain. They evaporate quickly if exposed to air or heat, and the light oils, like eucalyptus and orange, disappear faster than heavy ones, such as sandalwood and patchouli.

The common scents of smell

Since it took 5,000 years of learning to work out which essential oils do what, the medicinal benefits take a lifetime to master fully. But a little knowledge goes a long way, and the 20 oils chosen here are the pick of the pleasurable bunch and, if used as described, are harmless. They smell wonderful and are the perfect antidote to a hard and difficult day. They are meant to pamper rather than cure, to train our sluggish sense of smell and keep it in peak performance, and to make both you and your partner happier and healthier. After one whiff, all the benefits will be as plain as the nose on your face!

BASIL
(*Ocimum basilicum*)
Oil from: flower top and leaves
Native of Asia, now grown from Europe to the Seychelles

Known as sweet basil, it has a piercing fresh smell with a hot and cold feel on the skin. The Greeks, Romans, and Egyptians used it constantly as a general healing cure-all. The leaves are mildly antiseptic, take the pain out of insect stings and sprigs are worn behind the ears in Spain and other places in Europe to keep buzzing and biting insects at bay. The essential oil has strong effects on the mind: it is refreshing, uplifting, increases confidence, and clears the head — so it is particularly good for headaches, anxiety, depression, and fatigue. Basil mixes best with geranium and frankincense.

CAMOMILE
(*Anthemis nobilis*)
Oil from: dried flowers
Grown in England, Morocco and Germany

Camomile is from the daisy family and is one of the oldest English medicinal herbs. It has a light aroma that is a mixture of apples and straw. The dried flowers steeped in hot water have been used as a hair rinse to make blondes blonder long before peroxide was even a twinkle in the hairdressers' eye.

German camomile has relaxing, calming, and sedative benefits, and contains azulene, a natural anti-inflammatory agent — so it is good for nervous tension, stress, insomnia, muscular aches, sunburn, skin complaints, and rashes. Camomile Maroc is good for itchy skin conditions. Camomile mixed with rose is particularly good for beating hangovers, and it also blends nicely with geranium or lavender.

CINNAMON LEAF
(*Cinnamomum zeylanicum*)
Oil from: leaves
Grown in Sri Lanka, Malaysia, and China

Cinnamon is so ancient it even gets a mention in the Old Testament. It has a pungent, spicy smell that is used to enliven everyone, from tired skiers (mulled wine) to hungry children (apple pie). The essential oil contains eugenol, a powerful antiseptic, and the spicy aroma is stimulating and an aphrodisiac — so it is equally good for colds, tiredness, and loss of libido. Cinnamon is so heady that it is best used alone, but it can be pleasant mixed with sandalwood.

CLARY SAGE
(*Salvia sclarea*)
Oil from: leaves
Grown in Southern Europe, West Asia, and the U.S.S.R.

Clary sage is a member of the sage family, with its distinctive pineapple scent. In Latin 'clary' means clear, and the name was used by the ancient Romans because they made a soothing eye lotion from the seeds of the plant. Clary sage should never be confused with sage (*Salvia officinalis*), which is one of the few toxic essential oils — it isn't recommended for home use and should never be applied during pregnancy. But the essential oil of clary sage has many excellent uses; it is a euphoric tonic, mildly antiseptic, and gently erotic — so it is good for depression, fatigue, general debility, and arousing emotions. Clary sage mixes well with lavender, jasmine, sandalwood, or ylang-ylang.

EUCALYPTUS
(Eucalyptus globulus)
Oil from: leaves
Native of Australia, now grown in Spain and the U.S.

Eucalyptus is one of the tallest trees in the world, with over 250 species. It has a strong, refreshing camphor smell, and a cooling effect on skin. For countless centuries, the Aborigines crushed the leaves to treat wounds and fight infection, and burned the branches on their fires to add to the flavour of roast lizard and other delicacies. The koala rates eucalyptus as its favourite feast and climbs up to 300 feet to reach the tenderest new leaves. The essential oil is a powerful antiseptic and kills airborne germs, as well as stimulating the nervous system and clearing the head – so it is good for fever, flu, colds, coughs, healing abrasions, soothing muscle aches, pains, and the sinuses. Eucalyptus is best used alone, but combines well with lavender.

FRANKINCENSE
(Buswellia thurifera)
Oil from: gum resin
Grown in East Africa and the Middle East

Frankincense has been valued for centuries and was burned to appease the gods as the earliest incense. It was so highly thought of that it made the ideal christening present (with gold and myrrh), delivered to Joseph and Mary in a Bethlehem stable. It has a sweet, spicy, woody smell, that improves with age. The essential oil is relaxing, rejuvenating, uplifting, and mildly antiseptic – so it is good for tiredness, grumpiness, negative moods, and emotions. Frankincense mixes well with basil, sandalwood, or lavender.

GERANIUM
(Pelargonium odorantissimum)
Oil from: leaves
Grown in France, throughout Europe and Africa

Geranium blooms in a riot of colours and takes over gardens in warm climates so that the air is filled with its sweet, fresh, soothing aroma. The petals, mixed with boiling water and a little brandy, make one of the most delicate toilet water perfumes. The essential oil acts as both a tonic and sedative on the nervous system, and, as it is antiseptic, it soothes and heals skin – it can put you to sleep or put you in a good mood, and will cleanse, refresh, and balance any complexion. It is the best essential oil for relieving anxiety. Geranium mixes well with all oils, but balances extra specially with rose or patchouli.

JASMINE
(Jasminum officinale)
Oil from: flower
Grown in France, Morocco, Algeria, Egypt, and China

There are more than 200 varieties of jasmine, with varying sized flowers in red, yellow, or white. It has one of the most romantic aromas, rich, exotic, sensual but not overpowering, and it is used in all the great classic perfumes because of its effect on men and women alike – which probably explains why Marilyn Monroe boasted that she wore only Chanel No 5 (with its strong jasmine note) in bed. The essential oil is uplifting, relaxing, and an aphrodisiac – so it is good for changing your mood and emotions in the gentlest way. Jasmine mixes well with most other oils.

JUNIPER
(Juniperus communis)
Oil from: dried berries
Grown in Canada and throughout Europe, particularly Yugoslavia

Juniper is what adds the flavour to gin and liqueurs like Chartreuse, and both the berries and leaves have the same pungent bitter-sweet smell. For centuries it was burned to ward off evil spirits, and later the fumes were used in hospitals to kill germs. The essential oil is very antiseptic, and both stimulating and relaxing – so it is good for stress, fatigue, and lack of energy. It is also an excellent diuretic and helps stop fluid retention, as well as being good for oily skin and for treating greasy hair. (Juniper oil should not be used during pregnancy.) Juniper mixes well with sandalwood, rosemary, and lavender.

LAVENDER

(Lavandula officinalis)
Oil from: flowers, leaves and stems
Grown in England, the Mediterranean, and Tasmania

Lavender was a favourite of the ancient Romans, who wouldn't bathe without it (Latin *lavare* means to wash), and it remained popular until the twentieth century, making the most beautiful women more fragrant. It has a clean, fresh scent, and is used in everything from talcum powders to pot-pourri. It is the most commonly used essential oil and the most useful, because it combines the opposing qualities of being both a stimulant and a sedative – so it is good to relieve nervous tension, help you to sleep, calm and soothe, or refresh, restore, and repair. It is also a powerful antiseptic, and is good for aches and pains or healing anything, from burns and scars to infections. Lavender helps round out all other oils, particularly patchouli and rosemary.

LEMON

(Citrus limonum)
Oil from: rind of fruit
Grown in Florida, California, Brazil, and the Mediterranean

Lemon has migrated throughout the world and ended up on everyone's menu – from a wedge with fish to candied peel on top of cake. Pliny the Elder, a great Roman scholar, decided in about A.D. 50 that the juice should be used by pregnant women 'to stay the flux and the vomit'. It has been used to lighten hair colour and whiten skin, and its tangy citrus smell is unique. It is one of the most vitamin-rich essential oils and is a potent antiseptic, and astringent. It is refreshing, and stimulating, so it is good for waking up. Lemon is so aromatic that it doesn't mix well, except with neroli, geranium, or lavender.

Essential oils are not oily at all and come in a variety of delicate shades, from the vivid yellow of lemon to the deep burgundy of patchouli.

NEROLI

(Citrus bigarradia)
Oil from: flowers of bitter orange tree
Native of China and Japan, grown
throughout the Mediterranean

Neroli is named after Flavio Orsini, a sixteenth-century Prince of Nerola, whose second wife adored the perfume. But the Romans believed that their god Jupiter gave an orange to Juno (his sister!) when he married her, and orange blossom has been carried by brides ever since. Neroli comes from an orange tree that blooms and fruits all year round, for up to 80 years, and it is the main ingredient in eau de Cologne. The essential oil is an hypnotic sedative and antidepressant, and is relaxing and calming – so it it good for anxiety, nervous tension, and insomnia, and is particularly soothing on dry skin. Neroli mixes well with rose, jasmine, lemon, geranium, and lavender.

PATCHOULI

(Pogostemon patchouli)
Oil from: leaves and wood
Grown in South East Asia and India

Patchouli is a very ancient smell of the East. It first made it to the West in the nineteenth century, when it was used to impregnate Paisley shawls woven on the Scottish Isles and exported to Europe. And as a single smell it featured heavily from Woodstock to the local bistro as the hippie scent of love and peace. It has a heavy, sweet, musty aroma that is the potent base of many heady perfumes. The essential oil stimulates in small amounts, and sedates when used more generously – so it is good for keeping you awake, sending you to sleep, or arousing sexual response in between. Patchouli mixes well with rose, lavender, or geranium.

PEPPERMINT

(Mentha piperita)
Oil from: leaves
Grown in Southern Europe, the U.S. and Brazil

Peppermint was named for its peppery smell, by a man called John Rea, who discovered it in an English field in 1700. It belongs to the huge mint family, and is manufactured in even huger quantities because it is so popular as a food flavouring – in everything from ice-cream to toothpaste (where it has whitening as well as freshening properties). The essential oil is about a third menthol, which is why it invigorates, refreshes, clears the head, and helps numb pain – so it is good for mental tiredness, emotional lethargy, muscular pains, headaches, inflamed skin, indigestion, nausea, and PMT. Being very potent, peppermint should always be used sparingly, and mixes well with rosemary. It can cause skin irritation in strong concentrations.

ROSE

(Rose gallica officinalis)
Oil from: petals
Grown in many countries, but the best quality comes from Bulgaria, Turkey, and Morocco

A rose by any other name would still titillate the most jaded nose. Loved by the Greeks and Romans, adorning the shields of Persian warriors, a symbol of the fight for the English throne in the fifteen century, and even carried as a rosette by modern day sports' fans backing their team, the rose is all-powerful. And it makes one of the most powerful essential oils. It is a romantic and sensual aphrodisiac, it boosts your confidence, beats stress, tension and headaches, banishes wrinkles, puffiness, blemishes and many skin complaints, and even bothers to help the liver battle a hangover. It is an excellent oil for mature skin. Rose should be used often, in small doses, and mixes well with all oils.

ROSEMARY

(Rosmarinus officinalis)
Oil from: leaves
Grown throughout Southern Europe and the U.S.

Rosemary comes from the latin 'ros-marinus', or dew of the sea, because it loves sandy soil and thrives in sight of the shore. It has always been known to keep hair glossy and healthy. In the seventeenth century, when gentlemen followed the lead of King

Charles II and wore elaborate, curled wigs, they liked to believe it was a cure for baldness (taking the wigs off would have stopped hair loss more effectively because they stifled the hair underneath, and made it weak and thin). The essential oil stimulates the whole body and mind, it clears the head, invigorates, and refreshes – so it is good for all muscular aches and pains, apathy, listlessness, lack of concentration, and low spirits. Rosemary mixes well with lavender and peppermint.

SANDALWOOD
(Santalum album)
Oil from: heart of wood and roots
Grown in Malaysia, Java, Borneo, Australia, India, and China
Sandalwood is actually a parasitic tree that attaches its roots to other trees and grows slowly at their expense – on average, only an inch in diameter per year. By the time it reaches its thirtieth birthday, the best oil can be extracted from deep within its yellow wood. For centuries it has been burned as incense, and used on funeral pyres or in religious ceremonies, and today it is the base of most green or woody perfumes. The essential oil acts as a sedative and stimulant – so it is good for insomnia, stress, and loss of libido, and it is particularly effective in strengthening the immune system for overall health. It has an affinity with the bladder and is good for urinary problems. Mixed with lavender, it is good for treating dry, inflamed skin. Sandalwood mixes well with clary sage, juniper, cinnamon, frankincense, and ylang-ylang.

TEA-TREE
(Melaleuca alternifolia)
Oil from: leaves
Grown in Australia and New Zealand
Tea-tree was named by Captain Cook's sailors, who brewed the leaves in their kettles, presumably added milk and sugar, and drank it on their travels. Its amazing healing properties were used by the Aborigines and Maoris, but it is only recently that Australian researchers have proved how effective it is. Tea-tree has a spicy, hot, medicinal smell, and is a powerful, yet non-irritating, antiseptic, that kills germs 12 times more effectively than carbolic. The essential oil is now commonly available in the U.S., Britain, and throughout the Pacific; it is good for cuts, burns, stings, acne, athlete's foot, and almost any other infection, as well as helping skin build up a resistance to germs. It is especially good for treating yeast and fungal infections and may be used (well diluted) in the bath or in a douche for both thrush and candida. Tea-tree can be mixed with lavender, but is equally effective alone.

THYME
(Thymus vulgaris)
Oil from: leaves
A native of Southern Europe and North Africa
Thyme was loved by all ancient cultures, and grows like a weed even on arid, rocky ground. It is hated by fleas, moths, and all flying insects, and is burned indoors in most European countries to rid the home of pests. It contains thymol, a powerful antiseptic that is used in deodorants and gargles to kill germs. The essential oil is an excellent stimulant as well as anti-bacterial – so it is good for fatigue, anxiety, headaches, and skin inflammations. Thyme is most effective used alone, but should be used sparingly as it can irritate sensitive skin.

YLANG-YLANG
(Cananga odorate)
Oil from: flowers
Native of South East Asia and Australia, and grows in Madagascar
Ylang-ylang is often called the flower of flowers because of its long, draped, yellow petals and spicy, exotic jasmine scent. It is one of the most aromatic essential oils, and affects the emotions and mind more than the body. It is an exciting aphrodisiac that stimulates the senses, yet it has a relaxing, hypnotic effect. It is good for calming nervous tension, lifting negative moods, irritability, and loss of libido. Ylang-ylang mixes best with the other sensual oils like clary sage, jasmine, and sandalwood.

Do-it-yourself aromatherapy When it comes to choosing which essential oils to buy, the rule is be led by your nose. Some smells that your partner loves will remind you of something you hate, so trial and error is part of the adventure. Start with a small collection: the basics that mix with everything are geranium, jasmine, lavender, or rose; and some useful extras are eucalyptus, sandalwood, or ylang-ylang.

When you buy essential oils, don't try to sniff the store from top to bottom. Our noses tire easily and switch off when they are bombarded – which is why we are lucky enough to stop smelling manure after ten minutes in a farmyard!

Since our sense of smell is triggered mentally and physically, essential oils can be used in many different ways. The most therapeutic and pleasurable way is by massage (see page 70), because it uses touch and smell equally. As the oils are absorbed by skin, adding them to a bath (see page 97) is almost as effective. Or you can treat your feet by soaking them in a bowl of hot water and oil (see page 132). Also, because essential oils are so volatile, the fumes are easily inhaled so they are equally enjoyable when used to scent rooms (see page 73).

The best oils have the best effect, so try to buy pure, undiluted, high quality

Play sniff-and-tell with your partner to test how keen your nose is, and train it to recognize and enjoy more aromas.

extracts from a reputable source. Most are sold in 10ml or ½fl oz bottles, and that is enough to last for six months – any longer and they begin to degenerate. Always store them in a dark, cool place with the lid firmly screwed on, as they evaporate quickly. Never use essential oils without diluting them first; applying them neat to the skin doesn't increase their power, and it may give you an allergic reaction. Peppermint oil, for example, can cause irritation. In general, less is best, so always measure oils carefully using an eye dropper. And since the oils are absorbed slowly by skin and trigger healing that continues, try not to shower or bathe for at least three hours after you have used them.

Before you start experimenting, the other thing to remember is that the more you use your sense of smell, the better it becomes – we only lose it as we grow older due to laziness. Although some of the Great Noses of perfumery can recognize almost all of the 10,000 scents known to man, the rest of us mere mortals have a very limited repertoire. The best way to practise is to get your partner to waft a few common household products under your nose, with your eyes closed to stop cheating. Try toothpaste, coffee, pepper, nutmeg, any fruit, shaving cream, and whatever else is to hand, to see how clever you are. The more sensitive you become to smell, the more you will enjoy it. And practice will also help you develop an instinctive nose for knowing which essential oils work well together.

The aromatic touch

Some essential oils almost cancel each other out, others clash, and offend rather than perfume. Until you develop your own favourite combinations, stick to the basic recipes here. But the simplest rule when it comes to making original potions is to group similar smells together – floral, spicy, herby and musky are the main aroma groups, and your nose should be able to tell you which are which. For stress or tension, the soothers are: geranium, frankincense, jasmine, lavender, neroli, patchouli, rose, sandalwood, and ylang-ylang. For fatigue or tiredness, the energizers are: basil, cinnamon, lemon, peppermint, rosemary, and thyme. For lack of sensuality, the arousers are: cinnamon, clary sage, jasmine, neroli, patchouli, rose, sandalwood, and ylang-ylang. And the best antiseptics for all round health are: cinnamon, eucalyptus, juniper, lavender, lemon, peppermint, sandalwood, tea-tree, and thyme.

An aromatherapy massage works wonders – and even that is underestimating its power! You can use all the basic massage techniques from chapter one, but should add more sweeping strokes to generate warmth and help oil absorption, and less vigorous ones so that the aroma does the stimulating. All essential oils need to be diluted, and for massage you must mix them with a carrier oil such as soya, safflower, grapeseed, sunflower, or any other good lubricant (see page 20). For 25ml (1 fluid ounce) of carrier oil, add 7–9 drops of essential oil; for 50ml (2 fluid ounces), add 15–20 drops.

It is best to make small amounts so it is as fresh and potent as possible, and it is a good idea to add a little vitamin E because it is an antioxidant and acts as a natural preservative for several months. Use the contents of a vitamin E capsule, or a teaspoon of wheatgerm oil, which is also rich in this vitamin. You can buy glass bottles from a drugstore or chemist to keep aromatherapy mixes in, and since they normally have the capacity stamped on the base, it makes it all very much simpler. And if your concentrated essential oil comes in a bottle without an inbuilt dropper, use an ordinary squeeze-action eye dropper or pipette to measure, but make sure it is cleaned thoroughly and completely between recipes.

To take the trial and error out of your first aromatherapy massage, here are some tried and tested combinations. Most make up 25ml, which is plenty for a full body rub-over, and more than enough for

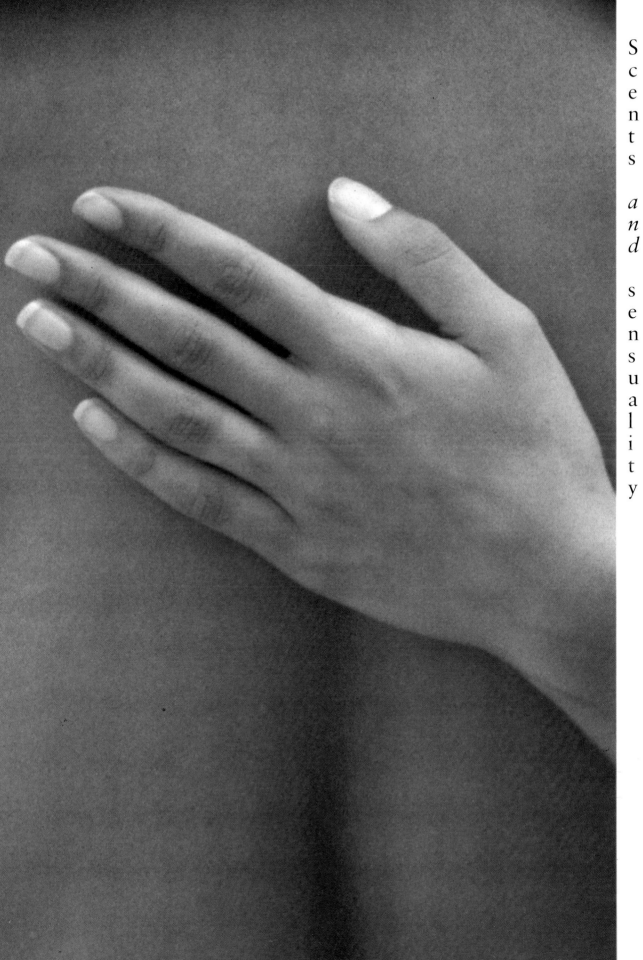

Scents *and* sensuality

three face or foot massages. They are cross-referred to the four step-by-step techniques in chapter one, to make it even simpler to decide which to use when. But bear in mind that the basic combinations work by pleasing your sense of smell, and so you should be led by your nose. If it is a recipe using three essential oils, such as rose, geranium, and lavender, get your partner to smell all three before you mix them; if lavender is his favourite, you may add an extra couple of drops of that so it is the top or most potent note, and less of his least favourite. It won't affect the basic balance of the aromatherapy treat, and it will give a more personal, intimate, and pleasurable feeling, rather than the chemistry set approach. So now all that is left is for you and your partner is to experiment and enjoy yourselves as much as possible.

Matching mood and massage

The following combinations of essential oils are particularly well suited for using with the massages described on pages 34–49 in The loving touch. They have been mixed so that you both can match them to your mood and particular need.

NECK, FACE, AND SCALP
The best essential oils for healthy hair are camomile to lighten fair hair or rosemary to add gloss to dark. Either of them mixed with lavender is soothing; use lemon or ylang-ylang for treating greasiness; for hair loss, use rosemary and lavender; and for dandruff, try rosemary or tea-tree. To treat just the scalp and hair, mix three drops in total with 10ml of carrier oil.

For an aromatic neck, face, and scalp massage to soothe fatigue and stress, use two drops each of rose, geranium, and lavender in 25ml of carrier oil; and for a sensual treatment use three drops of jasmine, three drops of rose, two drops of neroli (plus 25ml).

If your partner has oily skin, try a mix of three drops of geranium, three drops of

lavender, two drops of lemon (plus 25ml); for dry skin use four drops of jasmine, four drops of rose (plus 25ml); for sensitive skin use two drops each of camomile Maroc, geranium, and rose (plus 25ml); and for an anti-wrinkle mix use two drops of rose, three drops of sandalwood, three drops of frankincense (plus 25ml).

THE BACK
For a relaxing massage, try any of the following essential oil combinations, each mixed with 25ml of carrier oil: four drops of lavender, two drops of geranium, two drops of sandalwood; three drops each of rose, jasmine, geranium; three drops of camomile, two drops of lavender, three drops of geranium; two drops of lavender, three drops of ylang-ylang, three drops of geranium.

For a stimulating, energizing massage, use any of these combinations with 25ml of carrier oil: three drops of lavender, two drops of rosemary, one drop of peppermint; three drops of sandalwood, two drops of cinnamon, two drops of clary sage; two drops each of lemon, rosemary, lavender; four drops of rosemary, two drops of basil, two drops of clary sage.

For a sensual massage, use any of these combinations with 25ml of carrier oil: six drops of sandalwood, two drops of cinnamon; three drops of jasmine, three drops of rose, two drops of neroli; three drops of patchouli, five drops of rose.

THE FEET
For tired or aching feet, use: three drops of rosemary, and three drops of lavender (plus 25ml); for an uplifting, sensual foot massage, try three drops of ylang-ylang, three drops of jasmine, two drops of clary sage (plus 25ml).

To wake up the mind while massaging the feet, use four drops of any one of the following, mixed singly with 25ml of the carrier: basil, lemon, peppermint, rosemary. Use five drops of lemon (plus 25ml) for slow circulation and cold feet, and five drops of tea-tree (plus 25ml) for soreness or any fungal infections.

THE SENSUAL BODY MASSAGE

For an arousing massage use any of these combinations with 25ml of carrier oil: three drops each of ylang-ylang, sandalwood, rose; three drops of geranium, three drops of rose, two drops of patchouli; three drops of jasmine, three drops of rose, three drops of neroli; or two drops each of ylang-ylang, clary sage, sandalwood.

The pick of the aphrodisiacs are as sensual used alone. Try between six to nine drops (less is sometimes more effective) of any of the following with 25ml of carrier oil – cinnamon (heady, sensual), clary sage (arousing), jasmine (gently seductive), neroli (sharp and arousing), patchouli (musky, intimate), rose (gently romantic), sandalwood (warm, erotic), ylang-ylang (exotic, potent).

The aromatic smell

Scentuality, or using aroma to make you feel better, is just as pleasurable to the nose as massage is to the body. It goes beyond the power of ordinary perfumery, because essential oils are so pure they are actually absorbed through the lungs as you breathe. By simply inhaling the oil's potent vapours, you can clear your head, boost your self-confidence, relax, invigorate, or change your mood. If you or your partner are tired, a quick sniff of lemon oil instantly wakes you up, peppermint, rosemary, or basil help you concentrate on a difficult task, and rose soothes the most savage hangover. And some of the more floral oils make you feel as if you are enjoying the fragrance of a summer garden in full bloom – which gives instant euphoria all year round.

When you're not in the mood for massage, there are many other ways to use smell therapy. Try an instant air freshener by shaking a few drops of essential oil in a pint of distilled water and putting it in one of those pump-action sprays for misting house plants, then squirt around the house. Another simple way of using them is by pouring a few drops of the most floral oils into a bowl of dried flowers to make your own pot-pourri. You can leave your partner a fragrant note by placing a droplet of oil on a cotton puff and dabbing it on your writing paper. And since all essential oils are more volatile when warmed, try adding a few drops to a room humidifier, a pan of steaming water, or in a small saucer of water on top of a radiator. And if you have an open fire, sprinkle a few drops directly on the wood before lighting the fire, for a sizzling dose of aromatherapy. You can also impregnate candles by storing them with tissues steeped in essential oils for a few days in a plastic bag. Three drops of rosemary, lavender, or lemon oil on a wet sponge can be used to clean and scent the bathroom and kitchen. Six drops on a cotton ball, slipped inside the vacuum cleaner bag, keep the house smelling fresh.

To affect the psyche, use camomile, geranium, lavender, neroli, or ylang-ylang (depression); jasmine, juniper, patchouli (listlessness); basil, geranium, neroli, thyme (anxiety); neroli, rose, patchouli, sandalwood, ylang-ylang (loss of libido). To affect overall physical health and kill airborne germs, use eucalyptus, juniper, lavender, lemon, peppermint, sandalwood, tea-tree, thyme (disinfectant and antiseptic).

Some smells are definitely more pleasing to the opposite sex than others, so you can treat your partner by picking the right bouquet. Masculine favourites include: basil (for action, drive), cinnamon (stimulating, steadying), frankincense (earthy, relaxing), geranium (positive, intimate), jasmine (sensuality, desire), lemon (sharp, inspiring), neroli (refreshing, uplifting), patchouli (enticing, peaceful), and sandalwood (virile, sensual). Feminine favourites include: clary sage (heady, exciting) geranium (sweet, peaceful), jasmine (intimate, seductive), lavender (positive, uplifting), neroli (relaxing, enthusiastic), patchouli (sensual, stimulating), rose (positive, romantic), rosemary (calming, creative), and ylang-ylang (exotic, erotic).

Finally, remember that one of the most potent ways to use essential oils is inhalation, and this is particularly therapeutic. If you both want a speedy, special treat, try a facial sauna. Put a few drops of oil (up to four maximum) in a bowl of hot water, drape a towel over your head, and bend over the bowl, breathing in deeply. This is excellent for an instant pick-me-up after a hard day. For energy, try basil, cinnamon, lemon, peppermint (one drop), rosemary, or sandalwood; for intimacy and relaxation use clary sage, geranium, jasmine, neroli, patchouli, rose, or ylang-ylang. For colds, headaches, and head clearers, add basil, eucalyptus, peppermint, or rosemary. And since the steam opens pores and cleanses the complexion, use lemon for oily skin and geranium, lavender, rose, or sandalwood for dry skin. Adding essential oils to your bath is especially pampering, as they are absorbed by your skin and inhaled at the same time. (For a selection of bathtime 'recipes', see page 99).

The 20 essential oils recommended throughout are all therapeutic, pleasurable, and very safe to use – if used according to instructions. Check before using any other essential oils as they may not be so safe. Occasionally, an essential oil may irritate sensitive skin, and if this ever happens, stop using it immediately and rinse the skin with cold water. They don't mix well with bottled scents, so always wash off all perfumes and toiletries beforehand. And never apply undiluted essential oils directly to the skin.

A fresh approach

The smell of roses is intimate, soothing, and sensual, and affects both men and women in a positive way.

There are many natural beauty treatments that are simple, safe, and satisfying ways of indulging your partner. Making your own cosmetics from common kitchen ingredients is not only good fun, but also lets you pamper one another in a way that helps heal and soothe common ailments, from razor burn to aching eyes. You can whisk up a healthy face pack, a softening exfoliator, or a luscious lip salve in under 15 minutes if you know which ingredients to use. Many fruits, vegetables, and grains have amazing medicinal properties that have been known for years. However, recent research into the most effective ways of growing quality produce in huge quantities has revealed even more information on the vitamins, minerals, enzymes, and health benefits of even the humble potato plant. And when a 'new' discovery is made, such as the soothing, quick-healing aloe vera plant – which has been used for hundreds of years in South America to treat burns – it is taken so seriously that the cosmetic industry adds it to the latest products within a matter of just a few months.

Using this knowledge to make your own beauty aids is a much simpler process. You can prepare just enough for a single treatment, so you don't need to add unnecessary ingredients such as preservatives; you can use it from a mixing bowl, rather than paying for a frosted-glass jar and elaborate packaging; and you know exactly what is in it and what it is supposed to do, without having to decipher the pseudo-scientific gobbledegook found on most beauty product labels. Fresh ingredients, applied immediately, are more potent because the vitamins and minerals have no chance to break down or evaporate. And if you keep recipes simple, they will have a pleasant texture and colour, as well as smelling good enough to eat. In fact, fresh peaches or strawberries liquidized alone for a face pack, smell so deliciously sensual that they can trigger the pampering process even more powerfully than aromatherapy oils.

There are thousands of fruits, vegetables, grains, pulses, and herbs that have excellent medicinal or beautifying properties. But the best for anyone with a busy lifestyle and little time are those that have many different uses, are inexpensive, and are available in local supermarkets almost all year round. The really vital natural remedies are those potent enough

to work alone, so that you need spend little time preparing them, and can have as much time to enjoy them as possible. All the ingredients chosen here fit this criteria; they also treat the commonest hair and skin problems and combine with many of the therapies in other parts of the book. The lemon handcream is doubly pampering when you add it to a manicure (see page 135), the fig exfoliator applied before the face massage (see page 35) helps the skin absorb the oil more rapidly, and the potato eye lotion is more soothing if you lie back and enjoy it while doing the sleep tight technique (see page 140).

The top 20 home treats

Remember that fresh is best, so try to buy quality produce and only mix up enough for one application. Although you can keep most mixtures in the refrigerator for a couple of days, they will lose their smell and some of their potency. When applying face masks, always avoid the eye area, leave for up to 30 minutes to work, rinse off, and smooth moisturizer over the skin to finish the treatment.

ALMOND: The oil or ground meal of the nut has been used for centuries; the Queen of France ordered 500lb (227kg) of almonds in one year (1372) to keep her complexion beautiful and enticing for her husband, King Charles V. Almonds soothe, tone and soften skin. For a moisturizing bath, finely grind $\frac{1}{2}$ cup fresh nuts and simmer with 1 cup milk over low heat for 10 minutes. Leave to steep until cool, then add to a hot bath and soak in it for up to 30 minutes. For oily skin, especially blackheads, grind 2oz (50g) nuts in a blender and rub gently on damp skin as a facial scrub. Splash with warm water to rinse, and apply moisturizer afterwards. For a softening, tightening face pack, grind 2oz (50g) fresh almond nuts in a blender, then mix 3 tablespoons with enough natural yogurt or warm milk to make a thick paste. Set aside for 10

minutes, then apply to the face, and leave for up to half an hour until the mixture dries. Rinse off with cold water.

APRICOT: The fruit and kernel contain a nourishing oil, rich in Vitamin A, which improves the texture and elasticity of skin. For a soothing, tightening eye gel, work the skin and flesh of two fresh apricots in a juice extractor, then chill the juice in the freezer for about ten minutes. Mix 2 teaspoons apricot juice with 1 teaspoon cold milk. Pat it around the eyes using a soaked cotton ball. Leave to dry and it will tighten and moisturize the skin surrounding the eyes in one go.

AVOCADO: They have a 20 percent oil content, and are rich in Vitamins A and E, which are good for moisturizing skin and hair. For a rich conditioner, to treat a flaky scalp or dry hair, mash half a ripe avocado with 3 tablespoons olive oil, blending until completely smooth. Massage the paste into dry hair (see page 35 for massage techniques), then wrap a towel round the head and leave for an hour before shampooing out thoroughly. If you add 2 drops of essential oil of rosemary to the recipe, it will help encourage hair growth as well.

CAMOMILE: The dried flowers contain azulene, a natural, soothing, anti-inflammatory agent, which is excellent for skin or hair. For a toning lotion, to soothe razor burn, itchiness, or any skin irritation, steep 12 flower heads in $2\frac{1}{2}$ cups boiling water and leave until cool. Chill the strained infusion in the freezer for 10 minutes, then dab on the affected skin, and leave to dry. The flower heads may also be added directly to a hot bath. For a hair rinse, to treat an itchy scalp or to lighten blonde hair, put 2oz (50g) dried camomile, 1oz (25g) dried marigold, 1 tablespoon lemon juice, and $\frac{1}{2}$ cup apple cider vinegar in a saucepan. Simmer for 15 minutes, leave to cool, and mix with 2 cups warm water. Pour it through clean, wet hair, and rinse with cool water.

Once thought of as an aphrodisiac, the tomato, or love apple, is a fine beauty aid. Rich in vitamins, it makes a gentle face pack.

CUCUMBER: The skin and flesh of cucumbers are rich in Vitamin C, and mildly astringent, soothing and healing. For an oily skin toner, to reduce shine and tighten, chop a medium-sized, unpeeled cucumber and work it in a juice extractor. Chill the juice and wipe it on the skin with a soaked cotton ball. It is also excellent for sunburn.

FIG: Fresh figs are rich in carotene (used by the body to make Vitamin A), and contain a natural, softening enzyme. Their grainy flesh makes a good abrasive scrub to remove dead skin. For a skin softening exfoliator, to treat dull or oily complexions, mash a whole fig, skin and flesh, then drain off excess juice (keep it to drink or add to fruit salad). Smear the pulp on your face, and massage gently in small circles for five minutes, leave for five minutes, then rinse off. It may be used to scrub a spotty or blemished back before trying the Total Back Tonic (see page 104).

GARLIC: The cloves of garlic contain alkaline salts and sulphur compounds that are good for purifying the blood and clearing up blemished skin. And 1 teaspoon garlic honey helps soothe a sore throat. (Put 12 unpeeled garlic cloves in a jar and pour in enough honey to cover. Leave to steep for a week before using – it will keep indefinitely as honey is a natural preservative.) For a quick acne or spot treatment, to draw out and heal blemishes, crush 2 cloves garlic and mix with 1 tablespoon warm olive oil. Dab directly onto blemishes with a cotton bud and repeat often.

HONEY: Pure honey hydrates and softens skin, and is a powerful natural antiseptic (this is why a jar of honey keeps for years). For an excellent lip salve, melt 1 tablespoon honey with 1 teaspoon of beeswax, then add 2 teaspoons almond oil. Place in a small screw-top jar and shake until the mixture emulsifies, then leave to thicken before smearing on chapped lips. It will keep for up to three

months. For a moisturizing face mask, beat 1 egg yolk into 1 teaspoon olive oil for five minutes, then gradually whisk in 1 tablespoon honey. Apply to the face, leave for 15 minutes until dry, then rinse off with warm water.

LEMON: The juice and flesh of lemons are rich in Vitamin C, mildly astringent, and have a bleaching effect. For a blonde hair rinse, to lighten hair colour, mix the juice of 1 lemon with 2 cups warm water, and pour through clean, damp hair. Do not rinse out. For a soothing hand cream, to whiten nails and soften skin, finely grate the rind of 1 lemon and put aside. Squeeze the juice into a jug and add an equal amount of olive oil. Place in a saucepan and warm just enough to melt 2 tablespoons beeswax, whisking all the time. Put in a screw top jar with the lemon rind and shake until it cools and emulsifies. Store in the refrigerator. Rub it into your hands every night or use for a soothing manicure (see page 135).

OATMEAL: Oats are rich in protein and minerals and, when finely ground into meal, they make an excellent face pack for drawing out impurities and softening skin. For a deep cleansing mask, to treat blemishes and blackheads, mix 3 tablespoons finely ground oatmeal with enough natural yogurt to make a thick paste. Apply and leave to dry for at least 15 minutes before rinsing off. For particularly blemished patches, gently rub the dry mask off with a fingertip before rinsing.

ORANGE: As well as the fruit being rich in Vitamins C and A, the oil in orange rind is moisturizing, and the flesh is mildly astringent. For a mild face cleanser, especially for combination skins, finely peel an orange and dry the rind for two days in a warm place. Then pulverize it to a fine powder (use a blender) and mix with 1 heaped tablespoon almond meal. Pulp the flesh and juice of a fresh orange in a blender, then add enough to the powdered

Oatmeal mixed to a paste with natural yogurt is an excellent cleanser for blemished skin. It is particularly good for treating blackheads.

mixture to make a thick, soft paste. Apply to the face, avoiding the eyes, and leave for at least 15 minutes. Rinse off.

PAPAYA: Rich in Vitamin C, calcium, and potassium, the flesh of the papaya fruit contains an enzyme called papain, which speeds up the metabolic rate to burn off calories (good for dieters), and softens skin. For a dry skin exfoliator, to remove rough skin patches, purée the flesh of half a papaya in a blender until smooth, then empty into a bowl. Blend the black seeds for a few seconds until they are coarsely chopped, then put them in a saucer. Dab the fruit mixture on dry skin and leave for a few minutes. Then dip a damp cotton ball in the chopped seeds until it is coated, and rub it in circles over dry skin. This is good for elbows, knees, and rough patches or calluses on the feet (follow with a foot massage, page 43, or pedicure page 136).

PEACH: The flesh and juice of fresh peaches contain an enriching oil and moisturizing enzymes. For a nourishing face pack, to treat dry skin or soothe razor burn, work all but the stone of a peach in a blender until smooth. Pat on the skin with a cotton ball and leave to dry. Rinse off.

POTATO: This ordinary vegetable is high in fibre, and rich in protein, Vitamins B and C, phosphoric acid, and potash. The juice of the raw potato is anti-inflammatory and softens, tightens, and slightly whitens skin. For a gentle eye lotion, to wipe away puffiness and undereye shadows, grate half a raw, peeled potato, then leave it on a saucer until the juice collects. Drain it off, pressing the flesh as you go, and chill the juice before patting it around the eyes. Leave to dry, then rinse off. A slice of raw potato placed over a bruise helps take the blue-blackness out of skin.

SEA KELP: Powdered sea kelp (from health food stores) is rich in iodine, potassium, many other minerals, and Vitamins A and D. It is richly emollient,

and soothes and softens skin. For a nourishing face pack, to treat mature or dry skin, mix 2 teaspoons honey with 1 tablespoon olive oil, and warm gently in a saucepan. Stir in enough powdered sea kelp to make a soft paste. Apply to the face, leave to dry for 15 minutes, then rinse off. For a soothing, relaxing bath, add 4oz (125g) powdered sea kelp to the tub under hot, running water. Mix with your hand, and soak for half an hour.

STRAWBERRY: These are a good source of Vitamins C and E, and folic acid, and the juice is acidic, astringent, and contains a mild laxative enzyme. For a natural toothpaste, to help control plaque, crush 3 very ripe strawberries and, using a soft toothbrush, rub the pulp all over the teeth and gums for several minutes before rinsing. For an oily skin astringent, to control and reduce shine, pulp 4oz (125g) fresh, ripe strawberries, and leave the juice to drain off. Dip a cotton ball into the juice, and apply it directly to the skin. Leave to dry, and do not rinse off.

TOMATO: Rich in Vitamins A, B, and C, and mineral salts, the juice of fresh tomatoes is astringent, healing, and toning. For a cleansing face pack, to reduce pimples, blackheads, and open pores, blanch 2 fresh tomatoes, remove the skins, and purée the flesh and seeds in a blender. Mix 4 tablespoons tomato purée with enough oatmeal to make a soft paste, and apply to the face. Leave for half an hour, then gently rub or rinse off.

WATERMELON: The flesh and juice are rich in Vitamins A and C, and cooling, firming enzymes. $\frac{1}{4}$ cup watermelon juice mixed with 1 teaspoon lemon juice and a little honey helps reduce a fever. For a tightening, refreshing toner, to treat mature skin or to alleviate stress or jetlag, place the flesh of a slice of watermelon in a strainer, and press out all the juice into a bowl. Chill the juice and dab it all over the face with a cotton ball, leaving it to dry and the skin to tighten.

Down to a tea

The smell, taste, and benefits of many medicinal plants can be used at home in one other simple way: by brewing them up and making a healthy pot of tea for two. Herbal tisanes will quickly relax a tense body, help an insomniac sleep, soothe an upset stomach, act as a tonic and energizer, and cure dozens of other common ailments. All you need is the right herb, boiling water, and a teapot. Dried herbs (from health food shops) are more concentrated, and generally you need one tablespoon per cup; fresh herbs, just picked, need to be crushed or chopped to release the milder flavour, and you need at least three tablespoons per cup. Fresh herbs should be free from chemical sprays, so be careful if you use any that are growing wild (wash them thoroughly).

Herbal teas should infuse and steep for at least ten minutes to allow the hot water to draw out the goodness. The trick is to half fill the pot, leave it to brew, then top it up with fresh boiling water just before drinking so that the tea isn't tepid. Never add milk to herbal teas because it may curdle and ruin the flavour, but you can add a little sugar or a teaspoon of honey to sweeten them if you wish.

Unlike ordinary tea and coffee, there is no limit to the number of cups of herbal tea you can safely drink each day because it contains no caffeine. It has long been recognized that caffeine is a stimulant that provides a false burst of energy and ultimately increases stress. Sleeplessness, irritability, palpitations, shortness of breath, and shaky hands are only some of the problems caused by a high intake of caffeine. Recent research suggests that fertility problems in both men and women may be linked to caffeine intake, and scientists regularly downgrade the number of cups of tea and coffee regarded as safe. Current thinking now puts this figure as low as one cup of each. Herbal teas have no such known side-effects and those listed here are recommended as safe. However, under no circumstances should you take essential oils internally.

Here is a list of the most beneficial herbs for home tea treats:

BASIL soothing and helps calm nerves (for tension, anxiety)

CAMOMILE relaxing, calming, sedating (for insomnia, stress)

COLTSFOOT anti-inflammatory, expectorant (for coughs, catarrh)

ELDERFLOWER a diuretic, cleanser, and purifier (for fevers, cold, fluid retention)

GINSENG anti-depressant, general tonic, energizer (for lethargy, anxiety)

LAVENDER gently uplifting, soothing (for stress, depression, tiredness)

LEMON BALM soothing, relaxing, calming (for tension, anxiety)

MARJORAM relaxing, soothing, analgesic (for headaches, migraine)

NETTLE rich in iron and minerals, cleansing, soothes inflammation (for circulatory problems, rheumatism)

PARSLEY cleansing, mild diuretic, rich in Vitamin C (for tired feet or legs, fluid retention)

PEPPERMINT calms digestive system, clears the head, freshens breath (for cramps, indigestion, morning sickness, nausea, hangovers)

RASPBERRY LEAF balances hormones, affects uterus (for period pain, menopause)

ROSEMARY aids digestion, calms nervous tension (for stress, stomach cramps, flatulence)

Water *and* well *being* are a vital combination.

After oxygen, it is the most important thing we consume. It has no taste, smell, or colour, but still rates as the most potent elixir of life. Apart from sipping it, we see it everywhere – three-quarters of the Earth is covered in water. As well as splashing in it, we are steeped in it – two-thirds of our body weight is fluid.

We could survive for weeks eating only potato chips (five chips provide 80 calories, enough to maintain energy levels for one hour while sitting down), yet without water we would die in days, even though it doesn't contain a single calorie. And we don't even have to remember to top up our tanks; a warning light called thirst starts flashing when we are running low. The human body maintains a natural water balance by making us thirsty enough to drink an average of 3–5 (British) pints (2–3 litres) of liquid each day – more in hot climates. At least one pint of this evaporates each night while we sleep, or during the day, as we perspire to prevent our systems from boiling over. Another pint acts as a cleanser and helps flush out poisonous wastes. The rest is used to plump up every cell and lubricate all our moving parts. The skin alone, the largest organ at 2,750 square inches, must have a ten percent water content to remain flexible and supple.

All this happens every time we drink the greatest thirst-quencher in the world – a glass of water. But when we soak in it or play in it, water refreshes parts of the psyche no other fluid can reach. It cleanses, relaxes, and makes our spirits as buoyant as our bodies. It is the best escape from the pull of gravity and the pressures of the world. Water is a natural tranquillizer that soothes and calms our emotions as much as our muscles.

This might be because it wakes a primitive response dating back to a time when all life was ocean based, before the seas receded and there was land to walk on. According to a theory first proposed in the 1960s by Sir Alistair Hardy, a British academic, mankind was more likely to have evolved from an aquatic ape than from its terrestrial relative. This theory is supported by dozens of facts discovered by scientists in the last 30 years: human blood has chlorine, potassium, and sodium in the same proportions as the sea; our bodies, unlike those of land apes, are designed to float and have a sleek shape – smooth, insulated with fat, and without

thick fur; the only other mammals that have evolved to communicate on a basic cognitive level are still in the ocean (whales and dolphins); and, unlike other land mammals, we can close off our air passages so we don't inhale water when we dive (by constricting the trachea, holding the breath, and reducing lung capacity so we are less buoyant).

There are many other evolutionary and genetic similarities between humans and more watery creatures, but the real story of our creation is something we can only hypothesize about: it happened too long ago for us to know for sure. The only certainty is that water still affects us in very deep ways. When we are asleep we fantasize about it, from jumping over puddles to swimming across an infinite lake. Carl Jung, the Swiss psychoanalyst, believed that dreams reveal our innate memory or 'collective unconscious', with water symbolizing feelings and the flow of emotions. Sigmund Freud, the Austrian psychiatrist, believed that most of what ails us is symptomatic of repressed sexuality, and dreaming of water signifies the longest bath of our lifetime – the nine-month swim in our mother's womb. Either way, water is one of the most powerful reflections of the deepest levels of our unconscious mind. And it has as much influence there as touch and smell have on the subconscious.

Although the potential of mind-water therapy has not been fully explored, it will play an important part in our future well-being. Already a splash and a gurgle are being used to soothe the mind as much as the body. In Britain, psychiatrists have been treating emotionally disturbed patients 'aquatically' by adding the taped sound of waves and the salty smell of the ocean to therapy sessions, and these seem to make the patients more relaxed, happier, and more responsive. In France, they are using 'free floating' in large swimming pools to treat anyone suffering from stress; you strap on body floats, lie on your back, listen to ethereal music through underwater headphones, and

The buoyancy of water and the backwash, waves, and fluid resistance give the human body greater freedom than it enjoys anywhere else on Earth.

gradually sink into a euphoric state of tranquillity. And in the United States, it is now common to use 'flotation tanks' for relaxation. These were pioneered by the neurophysiologist Dr. John Lilly. You lie in silence in a dark tank, floating on a few inches of water mixed with enough Epsom salts to make it more buoyant than the Dead Sea, and escape from gravity and most other sensory experiences (sight, smell, sound). This seems to make the brain switch to releasing 'theta' wave patterns, which are deeply relaxing, and some people who have experienced flotation say that they have amazing flashes of inspiration and come out of the tank with all kinds of new ideas.

Water has been used for centuries to cleanse and soothe the body, by varying its temperature or relying on its wetness alone. But the latest research proves that its buoyancy has an equally important therapeutic value. The human body becomes almost weightless when floating in water, and we feel as if we are 90 percent lighter than we are on dry land. Every pool, stream, lake or sparkling seashore invites us to take the plunge. Once we are immersed, the spirit is buoyed up as much as the body, and we splash, swim, duck, and dive with childish abandon, before emerging – dripping, refreshed, and renewed. Water cradles the body so it relaxes, and caresses it with the force of waves, backwash, and fluid resistance. And this gives us a unique freedom that we enjoy nowhere else on Earth.

Exercising in water is exceptionally therapeutic – the resistance makes it effective, while the buoyancy means it seems effortless. Muscles can be stretched and extended without strain, and joints are mobilized without the shock of impact on solid ground. This is why modern water therapy has developed way beyond pure pleasure. Today, race horses paddle to prepare for the turf, athletes train in pools for the Olympics, there are aquatic classes for pregnant women, aquarobic workouts with strap-on weights for fitness fanatics, and dozens of physiotherapy programmes for the elderly, handicapped, or injured.

The other main use for water is washing. Basic hygiene would be impossible without H_2O molecules – they make up the finest solvent in the world, gently dissolving all dirt and grime on the outside of the body. Although we add soap, water alone will rinse off the million varied bacteria living happily in every human armpit. In fact, alkaline soap can neutralize the skin's acid mantle, which helps defend naturally against bacterial invasion. There is a theory that we have become obsessive about personal hygiene in the last 30 years – mainly as a result of the dozens of products the cosmetic industry has created in its attempts to shape consumer 'needs'. The average household contains soaps, toothpaste, deodorant, mouthwash, aftershave, perfume, talcum powder, foot spray, breath freshener, and a douche – all to keep us sweet and fragrant. Remember that, although they all make personal hygiene more enjoyable, none of them works without water, and just rinsing with warm water leaves us feeling refreshed, clean, soft, and sensual.

The other place that benefits from a daily dose of water is the face. It plumps up fine lines, and acts as the best anti-wrinkle moisturizer ever invented. This is why every tub of cosmetic softening cream you buy is 30–50 percent water, and emollient lotions contain a staggering 70–80 percent. It is the water, rather than anything else these products contain, which actually softens skin. Most other ingredients either hold water in the skin by laying down a sealing barrier (emollients, i.e. oils), attract extra water molecules (humectants, i.e. glyceride), bind one chemical to another, give a smoother consistency, or preserve shelf life. Even though a moisturizing product can keep skin softer by topping up its water content, it can't do it indefinitely. As we age our skin thins, sags and dries out, so even the most expensive moisturizers are not a source of eternal youth.

Having someone else shampoo your hair helps rub away tension all over the head and scalp as effectively as having a massage, as well as removing dirt and grime and making your hair shine.

On the water front

The simplest forms of water therapy, which date back thousands of years to the ancient Romans and Greeks, are all based on its cleansing and stimulating effects. They use a combination of hot and cold soaking to dilate and constrict blood vessels (increasing the circulation), and open and close pores in the skin (evaporating wastes out of the body). The ritual of bathing has always been for pleasure, relaxation, and pampering.

Compared to the ancient world, we enjoy water on a very basic level; 5,000 years ago they lingered in opulent tubs for hours at a stretch in the most decadent way. By 3000 B.C., there were bathrooms in Mesopotamia that make those in the latest glossy soap opera seem spartan; they were bigger than most modern apartments, had footbaths, hot and cold tubs, and marble and gold fittings. The Greeks, who were such body worshippers they would have put Jane Fonda to shame, built baths and gyms together, with steam rooms next to plunge pools. And the Romans, who thought cleanliness was next to godliness, criss-crossed Europe with giant aqueducts for supplies of running water; the longest one is the Acqua Marcia that stretched 57 miles (92km), with only 7 miles (11km) above ground. By the fourth century B.C. there were over 900 public baths in Rome alone, and they were used socially (for orgies or business meetings), as well as being the first recorded example of a fast food chain (floating trays of snacks were mandatory).

The barbarians of the Dark Ages put a damper on all these civilized developments; to them, Roman plumbing was completely incomprehensible and it was left to decay and fall apart. Drainage wasn't included in the city of London until 1865, and it was only built to stop the spread of disease, rather than to supply indoor plumbing. And four years earlier, when it was announced that a bathroom was being installed in the White House, there was a public outcry throughout the United States at such unnecessary expenditure. The Victorian idea of hygiene was very basic, and until the end of the nineteenth century, the idea of a shared family bathtub was considered faintly disgusting – once a fortnight you retired to your own room to freshen up with a pitcher of hot water, a pitcher of cold water, and a shallow metal tub.

For centuries, the only place to enjoy running water was in a river, stream, by the seashore, or at one of the many health spas dotted around Europe. These spas, built around natural mineral springs, were a reduced version of the Roman approach, when bathing was used for pleasure and therapy. King Charles IV of Spain liked the cure at Carlsbad, Queen Victoria preferred Aix-les-Bains, Napoleon retreated to Vichy, and thousands of others went with ailments from gout to consumption. By the twentieth century, therapies included treats as dangerous and unpleasant as electric baths and slime chest poultices. However, the spa water itself did nothing but good.

We now know why: not only is underground spring water pure and fresh, but it picks up minerals and trace elements from the layers of peat, clay, and rock it seeps through: mainly potassium, calcium, sulphur, magnesium, sodium, copper, iodine, and iron. These are absorbed in minute amounts through our skin or in larger quantities when taken internally, and are all vital for a healthy body. Today, you can drink glasses of water from the same source almost anywhere in the world – bubbling bottles of pure moisture have become part of our health-conscious lives. There are more than 50 springs in France alone, each exporting under a different designer label and brand name, with some of them costing more per litre than oil when they reach their destination. And taking the waters abroad by bottle has meant that a lot of the most famous European springs now run into factories rather than plunge pools.

From swallowing a glass of water to soaking, swimming or playing in it: all contact with H_2O helps refresh parts of the psyche no other fluid can reach.

Spa-ing partners Perhaps the ultimate way of pampering your partner (and yourself) is to take time out together for a weekend break and visit a spa, health farm, or fitness centre. They offer dozens of high-technology treatments using the latest equipment to make water totally therapeutic. An average two-day stay will be action packed with pampering, and both of you will come home feeling as if you have had a much longer respite – fitter, stronger, relaxed, re-energized, and raring to go.

Many health spa therapies use water, and may be adapted to enjoy at home, from beautifying sea mud and kelp treatments to relaxing hot steam, cold plunges and water jets or whirlpools.

Health spas aren't cheap, but they do you more good than a week's break anywhere else. It is known that stress doubles as you plan a holiday (Where will we go? Have we packed everything? Who has got the tickets? Who will feed the cat? Did we lock the back door? etc.). Going to a spa is simple by comparison; almost everything is provided, most guests only wear casual track suits, and once you get there you don't have to think about anything until you leave. This total escape from anxiety and stress is what you are paying for.

You also have the chance to enjoy the pleasures of dozens of treatments that are often too expensive, messy, or time-consuming for home use. Moreover, you can both enjoy them simultaneously. To give you an idea of some of the treats that are available at health spas worldwide, here is a list of the best of the ancient therapies that have survived the test of time, and the pick of the latest ones that are the result of modern technology. Where suitable, suggested adaptations for home use have been included. While these are not always as luxurious or therapeutic as professional spa treatments, they do offer a way of pampering your partner that is both beneficial and economic.

AQUAROBICS: Supervised classes in the spa pool using a series of water exercises to strengthen and tone muscles. Many sessions now include strap-on weights or floats to make the workouts even more effective. For a series of simple exercises that you and your partner can enjoy doing together, see pages 106–109.

BODY WRAPPING: A series of treatments designed to cleanse the body and reduce weight by perspiration. Hot gels, lotions and plant extracts are applied, then you are wrapped in foil or cloths to encourage sweating.

Home treatment versions of body wrapping are not recommended. Not only is the procedure difficult and messy, it can be unsafe in the hands of an amateur, resulting in severe burns.

FACIALS: Herbal or plant extracts are applied to the face, often with massage, and then steam, poultices, or high frequency currents are used to speed up skin absorption.

Most spa or salon facials cannot be reproduced at home, as they often require expensive, specialist equipment and trained beauticians. Applying a facial mask, however, is quite safe (and inexpensive), and gives you the chance to relax and unwind while it works.

Masks may be used to cleanse, exfoliate, stimulate the circulation, or soothe and soften the skin. Many different kinds are available commercially, and you can also make your own from natural ingredients (see page 74). You can, of course, use two different kinds of masks to suit combination skins.

Whatever type of mask has been chosen, application follows the same basic routine. Tie your partner's hair back, if necessary, and make her comfortable, leaning back in a chair or lying down, with her head and shoulders resting on a towel. Cleanse her skin (neck and face, or just her face, depending on the type of mask). Gently apply her usual toner on a cotton pad. Apply the mask, according to the manufacturer's instructions, keeping well clear of the eyes and mouth. A spatula is sometimes supplied, but using your hands is more sensual. Work gently and smoothly from the neck, across and up to the edges of the face. Cover your partner's eyes with cotton pads soaked in a soothing eye lotion or plain, cold water. Leave the mask for the time specified; this is a good opportunity to listen together to your favourite (quiet) music. You could even let your partner apply a mask to your face and then lie semi-supine relaxing together. If you are feeling especially loving and pampering, you could use the time usefully to give your partner a manicure (see page 135), a pedicure (see page 136), or a foot massage (see page 43).

When the appropriate time is up (do keep an eye on the clock), either peel or rinse off the mask, depending on its type. Pat the skin dry with a clean, soft towel. Apply toner to close the pores and finish by gently smoothing on moisturizer.

FANGO: All manner of mud treatments are used to re-mineralize skin and draw out impurities. They usually include warm mud baths, body wraps, and facials.

It is difficult but possible to give your partner a full body mud treatment at home, and a selection of commercial mud products is available for treating the face or breasts. Make sure you buy organic mud, which is rich in mineral and vegetable extracts. Use it to cleanse, soften, and exfoliate the skin, as well as to soothe both mind and body. As with facials, the treatment can be made more luxurious by playing music or reading aloud while it is taking effect. Perhaps the most pampering act is to clean up and wash the towels afterwards.

MASSAGE: You can choose from a selection of specific or all over body rubs, manipulation, and pressure. At spas they may be done by hand, vibrating pads, body brushing, ultrasound (short sound waves for vibration), or electrical pulses (to twitch individual muscles).

RELAXATION TECHNIQUES: These include breathing, meditation, yoga, rolfing, visualization, or the Alexander principle (see glossary, page 141). These are all taught in classes so that you can learn how to overcome stress.

SAUNA: Developed hundreds of years ago in Finland, saunas are now used worldwide. It is a dry heat treatment using a stove in a small, wood-lined room to raise the body temperature and increase perspiration. Saunas should be followed by a cold shower or plunge to invigorate and to close the pores. This is a spa treatment that can sometimes be shared by you and your partner. However, the sexes are often segregated in public saunas.

SCOTCH DOUCHE: Used in Europe for more than 50 years, this treatment involves strong jets of hot and cold water sprayed up and down the back to stimulate the spinal nerves and blood flow throughout the body. It is commonly adapted in many ways – from seawater sprayed on the thighs to remove cellulite to a form of massage from top to toe.

If you are lucky enough to have a pulsating shower, you can adapt this treatment for home use. Make sure the bathroom is at a comfortable temperature and that you have plenty of warm, dry towels to hand. Get in the shower with your partner so that you can control both the temperature and the direction of the jet. Remember that spraying cold water over him may not strike your partner as being very pampering, so be judicious in your handling of the temperature control.

For those who do not have a pulsating shower, The sponge lunge on page 103 is a gentler and simpler version.

SEAWEED TREATMENTS: These include a range of therapies using dried and powdered seaweeds, which are rich in vitamins and minerals similar to those in human blood, to improve health. Seaweed is used in hot baths, facials, body wraps, and many other techniques. A range of seaweed based products, from shampoos to bath foams, is commercially available.

SITZ BATH: This treatment, originally from Germany, uses two tubs, one filled with hot, the other with cold water, to cleanse the body. Usually the feet are in one tub, the torso in the other and the temperature of the water is reversed so that blood goes quickly from top to toe.

This is not really a practical spa therapy to adapt for home use. A reduced version would be a footbath (see page 132), using warm and cold water alternately.

STEAM THERAPIES: These offer a selection of treatments using wet, steaming heat to create greater perspiration and cleansing than dry heat. Steam is used for facials, body wraps, in rooms (like the sauna), or with body cabinets that leave the head exposed (similar to the Sitz bath). For an aromatherapy steam facial, see page 74.

TURKISH BATHS: Wet steam heat opens the pores, and this is followed by a cold plunge to invigorate. An all over body brush and massage in between relaxes and cleanses the body.

WHIRLPOOLS: Pioneered in the last 20 years, whirlpool treatments use the action of water – with strong jets or bubbles – to massage and relax the body. These are also known as hut tubs and Jacuzzis.

This is one of the few spa therapies you can share, rather than being treated simultaneously but separately. The warm bubbling water evokes a similar response in mood, making you feel light-hearted.

Most of these techniques have now been adapted into modern, portable units – from facial steamers to whirlpool attachments – so we can enjoy them at home, rather than at the spa. Even the commoner types of bath therapies are now more accessible than their ancient equivalents, thanks to modern technology. Just 40 years ago, the average American bathroom measured 5ft × 7ft and contained a basin, toilet, and bathtub; today, it has more than doubled in size, there are two basins, a tub, a shower unit, and a separate toilet. In the 1950s, the British, who have always preferred horizontal ablutions to the upright shower, took one bath per person each week, whereas today, 60 percent of women and 45 percent of men enjoy a daily bath. (For some reason, British men soak for two minutes longer than women, who get out after an average 24 minutes!) We have dozens of different kinds of showers (pulsating massagers, adjustable pressure, fine or waterfall jets), and baths (whirlpools, sunken tubs, Jacuzzi spas), and all of them make water more pleasurable and therapeutic.

Although you might not have the luxury of your own Jacuzzi or swimming pool (but they are ideal for pampering, if you have), there are dozens of ways to make the ordinary bathtub work miracles for a tired, aching body. A warm bath is the simplest way to relax and unwind after a hard day. Cold water stimulates, and hot water soothes and sedates, so the combination of both (if you can bear it) is doubly effective. Once you start adding extra ingredients to the water, you can enjoy a different type of bath every day of the week. There are many ways of using water to promote well-being and pamper your partner at the same time. The best aren't complicated or time consuming, and they can be enjoyed in the privacy of your own bathroom without having to install the latest in hi-tech plumbing accessories. All you need is a tub, hot and cold water, and of course, your partner.

Bathtime basics Getting into the tub together or treating your partner to some special pampering makes the simple task of getting clean much more fun, sensual, and intimate. Double the pleasure by creating a luxurious atmosphere. Bathing by candlelight is delightfully romantic. Set the mood with a sensual essential oil in an oil burner; try jasmine, rose, or ylang-ylang. Tune into some gentle music, take off your clothes and get in.

The bath is a tranquil oasis in an otherwise mad world. It is so relaxing that it is one of the few places left where we are not embarrassed to burst into song! The gurgling water and steam, combined with a warm soak, banish anxieties to the extent that it is possible to contemplate nothing beyond one's own navel. But all of these simple pleasures are invariably forgotten in the frantic rush to get up, get washed, and get ready for the day ahead.

Only the Japanese still look upon bathing as an art form rather than a necessity; they rinse and lather once to cleanse the body, then run fresh, hot water and soak neck-deep to cleanse and restore the soul. A quick shower fills them with horror, and although it is a fast, efficient, and hygienic way to wash, it rates zero on the pure pampering scale.

The most luxurious bathtime treats should be long, slow, and as soothing to

A long soak in a hot tub is relaxing, pampering, and pleasurable, while quick dips are meant for cleanliness only: if you separate the two types of bathing, you'll get the best from both.

95

the mind and body as possible. The best time to indulge is after a hard day's work, when we need to be restored and refreshed from top to toe. And if you and your partner separate your water sports into necessities (cleanliness) and pleasures (pampering), you will get the best from both types of bathing, as well as occasionally being able to combine them in a wonderfully self-indulgent way.

The temperature of the water sets the tone for any bath – very cold or very hot water means a quick dip of about ten minutes. Tepid or warm water means anything from 15 minutes to hours of soaking, if you've got the time and don't mind emerging with prune-wrinkled feet. If you want an invigorating, energizing effect use stimulating, cool water (65°F–75°F/18°C–24°C); tepid water (75°F–85°F/24°C–30°C) has a relaxing, soporific effect and will help you sleep soundly; warm water (85°F–95°F/30°C–35°C) is the most deeply relaxing and helps take the ache out of tired bodies; and hot water (higher than 95°F/35°C) is slightly debilitating, and leaves you feeling floppy and deeply relaxed. If you want to be precise, check the temperature with a thermometer while running the bath and adjust it before it is full. As very hot water makes the heart beat faster and sends blood rushing around the body, it can be dangerous for anyone recovering from an infection, the elderly, and those with heart problems; if in doubt, seek medical advice beforehand. As alcohol dilates the blood vessels almost as much as very hot water, it is a mistake to combine the two – you'll end up with an exhausted, fainting drunk on your hands! However, a glass of wine with a tepid or warm bath is quite safe, and can make it more relaxing and enjoyable if

you are trying to unwind after a stressful and exhausting day.

The other basic requirements for a truly pampering bath are comfort and atmosphere. The room should be warm, no matter the time of year, so that you don't become chilled. Soft lighting rather than harsh fluorescent tubes will help make it more intimate and more of an escape from the real world. Serious bathers add a good book, an inflatable neck pillow, a portable cassette player with familiar tunes to sing along to, and a few simple snacks on the side as an extra indulgence. And since nobody has yet invented an all-over, hot-air body drier, large, warm towels within arm's reach are essential, whether you are taking a quick cold dip or a steamy sensual soak.

Beyond these basics, everything else you add just increases the pleasure. The main thing to remember is that warm water soothes a tortured body. You can use a bath to put you in the right frame of mind for any of the other treats in this book, so when you get home in the evening, have a bath before you do anything else. Massage is even more indulgent after soaking in a tub; warm water starts loosening muscles so they are relaxed before your partner even lays a hand on you. And when skin is immersed in water, it loses some of its own natural lubrication and dehydrates, so that massage oil is drawn into the skin and absorbed more rapidly immediately afterwards. Essential oils added to water penetrate more deeply as well, through body tissue and by being inhaled. Even exercise is easier after a bath because joints and ligaments are warmed, which makes them supple and flexible. Here are some surprisingly simple ways of using water to increase your well-being.

Essential aquatherapy They say Cleopatra bathed in asses' milk, and Mary Queen of Scots soaked in wine. Modern bath additives are less extravagant, but equally unusual: you can buy dried mud or seaweed extracts, bubbling gels infused with herbs, fragrant foams, and milky lotions. Although they all make bathtime more fun, many of them contain added ingredients to make the products more appealing; synthetic detergents, perfumes, colourants, thickeners, stabilizers, and preservatives are commonly used by manufacturers.

However, these ingredients are often unnecessary, and they may increase the risk of skin irritation or allergic reactions.

When you add essential oils to your bath, you know exactly what is going into the water. They are pure, simple, and pleasant to use. They soak into skin, are inhaled with every breath, and help soothe mind and muscle simultaneously. And because essential oils are so volatile, the warm, steamy water releases more aroma molecules in the room than when you use them for massage. This means that the smell is potent, pleasurable, and extra powerful.

The best way to use essential oils in the bath is to add them drop by drop, after you've turned the taps off, so that they float on the surface of the water and, as you step in, mix and lightly coat your skin all over. Make sure the bathroom door is closed before adding oils, so that none of the scent escapes, and be ready to jump straight into the tub. The tiny molecules will evaporate into the air for more than 15 minutes, but your nose will register them less and less, as it 'tires' and switches off the smell. Don't be tempted to add more oils after a few minutes – the initial droplets will keep working long after your nose is oblivious to them. Essential oils are potent: smaller doses are often more effective than larger ones, and using them undiluted may irritate sensitive skins.

In general, the maximum needed for a single bath is eight drops, although some specific oils require fewer. The therapeutic benefits are the same as when you apply essential oils during massage, but because you're relying more on your sense of smell than touch, some oils are better in the bath than others. To refresh your memory, an instant checklist of which oils are good for what, plus the maximum number of drops of each oil that you should add to a bath is given on page 98. When using a single aroma, the only other thing you need add is water.

Any of these essential oils used alone will have the desired effect, but remember that the aromatherapy is more noticeable in a steamy bath than the aquatherapy. If you are tense and over-stressed, don't choose a relaxing essential oil – choose the one that most stirs your senses when you sniff it. Always be led by your nose, because if you're affected positively by a smell trapped in a bottle, you'll be affected a hundred times more when it's released in your bath. You will love some oils for ever, some for only a few weeks before tiring of them, and others only at certain times of the year. Sharp or floral bath aromas are refreshing in summer, while musky, woody smells are comforting during the cooler winter months. As long as you let yourself be guided by your nose, you simply can't go wrong.

Using several oils at a time gives the bath a fragrant bouquet that stimulates the senses even more powerfully than when they are used singly. Although the aromas combine, the individual oils seem to keep their own notes: a waft of one is followed by another, and the scents merge and separate in waves. It is like closing your eyes, burying your nose in a bouquet of flowers and noticing the fragrance as a whole, while at the same time being able to name every bloom in the bunch. This effect is due to the warmth of the bath water. Heat increases the impact of any aroma, which is why the smell of fresh cut grass fills the air in summer, but hardly

ESSENTIAL OIL	THERAPEUTIC EFFECT	DROPS
BASIL	Energizing, invigorating, and refreshing	3
CAMOMILE	Relaxing, soothes aches and itchy skin	5
CINNAMON	Stimulating, uplifting, heady	6
CLARY SAGE	Arousing, invigorating, gently erotic, and uplifting	6
EUCALYPTUS	Relaxing and for muscle aches, colds, and flu	7
FRANKINCENSE	Rejuvenating, soothing, relaxing	7
GERANIUM	To put you to sleep or put you in a good mood	8
JASMINE	Erotic, exotic, and soothing	8
JUNIPER	To boost energy and beat stress (not during pregnancy)	5
LAVENDER	Stimulant and sedative, calming, refreshing, restoring	8
LEMON	Wakes up the mind and body, stimulating, arousing	5
NEROLI	Hypnotically soothing, good for tension and anxiety	8
PATCHOULI	Stimulating, erotic, arousing	8
PEPPERMINT	Invigorates, refreshes, warms, and energizes	3
ROSE	Seductive, romantic, soothing, and calming	6
ROSEMARY	Energizing, invigorating, and clears the head	5
SANDALWOOD	Heady, sensual, deeply soothing	7
TEA-TREE	Healing, calming, good for aches, abrasions, and fungal infections	8
THYME	Uplifting, invigorating stimulant, good for stress or anxiety	5
YLANG-YLANG	Sensual, seductive, deeply relaxing	7

gets beyond the compost heap in winter. When using more than one oil per bath, there is no need to mix them together beforehand. Just add them drop by drop to the surface of the water, and stir them up as you step in. You may use up to three different essential oils at a time; any more and the smells will start clashing and confuse your nose. But no matter how many oils used, make sure the total number of drops never exceeds eight per bath, or fewer depending on individual potency. (Refer to the chart opposite for maximum drops per oil.) To inspire you to create some of your own bathtime brews, here are some perfect essential oil combinations that pamper the nose as much as the body.

ENERGIZING BATHS

For the perfect pick-me-up when fatigued, weak, or tired, try the following combinations in summer or whenever the weather is hot: six drops of lavender, two drops of lemon; two drops each of basil, clary sage, thyme; two drops of peppermint, four drops of rosemary; three drops each of basil and rose.

For a warming, invigorating pick-me-up in winter and colder weather try: two drops of juniper, four drops of lavender, two drops of sandalwood; four drops each of cinnamon and sandalwood; two drops each of juniper, peppermint, rosemary; four drops each of lemon and thyme.

RELAXING BATHS

These soothing combinations are the best antidote to stress or tension – you will step into the water feeling uptight and step out feeling tranquil. In summer use: four drops each of camomile and lavender; four drops of geranium, three drops of jasmine, one drop of patchouli; four drops each of neroli and rose; four drops camomile and four drops geranium. In winter try: two drops of frankincense, three drops of sandalwood, three drops of ylang-ylang; four drops each of eucalyptus and lavender; two drops of geranium, four drops of patchouli, two drops of rose.

SEDUCTIVE BATHS

These are the pick of the particularly sensual combinations, using oils which arouse the mind and stir up the emotions. They are heady, exotic, intimate blends that are impossible to ignore.

In summer try: two drops of jasmine, three drops of neroli, three drops of rose; four drops each of neroli and ylang-ylang; two drops of clary sage, three drops of jasmine, three drops of ylang-ylang.

In winter use: two drops of clary sage, three drops of sandalwood, three drops of ylang-ylang; four drops each of rose and patchouli; three drops of cinnamon, three drops of sandalwood, two drops of ylang-ylang; five drops sandalwood and one drop geranium.

For a masculine combination treat him to three drops of cinnamon, two drops of frankincense, three drops of sandalwood; for a feminine combination treat her to two drops of clary sage, three drops of jasmine, three drops of ylang-ylang.

THERAPEUTIC BATHS

Remember that a lavender or camomile bath will soothe sunburn, camomile is good for itchy skin and allergies, eucalyptus is the best head clearer when you have a cold or sinus problems, tea-tree is excellent for fungal infections (including thrush), and rose works wonders for the most savage hangover (especially if you wrap some ice-cubes in a towel and use it as a neck pillow while soaking in the bath).

Other therapeutic oils that may be added to the bath include lavender for headaches; ylang-ylang for depression; clary sage for PMT and menstrual problems; frankincense, neroli, geranium, or lavender for anxiety; juniper and rosemary for fluid retention; the same combination (juniper and rosemary) for cellulite; and geranium, lavender, or sandalwood for overcoming the effects of travel, especially jet lag.

For extra information on all of the essential oils mentioned here, refer to scents and sensuality (pages 62–67).

The rub-a-dub-tub Before you even step in a bath of water, you can get your partner to pamper you with a dry friction massage. This is warming, relaxing, and stimulates the body's own cleansing system by stirring up the flow of blood and lymph. It also helps rub off the outer layer of dull, dry, dead skin, so that the living layer below glows healthily. We replace our entire skin surface 20 times a year quite naturally by shedding approximately one million dead cells every 40 minutes.

Although that may sound fatal to the uninitiated, it is a miniscule amount of skin. If you spread 1.5 million cells in a single layer, they would barely cover a fingernail. These dead cells form part of the epidermis. They form a protective barrier against bacteria, ultra-violet light and other potential enemies to the living skin cells beneath. As they are shed, they are replaced by new cells migrating towards the skin's surface.

However, when these dead cells are left undisturbed, they tend to build up and cover the bloom or sheen of the living cells below, particularly in winter when we are more lethargic, or when the body is exposed to strong sunshine which dries out the top layer faster. A good, brisk rub all over instantly removes this build up and wakes up the body at the same time. It will leave you feeling invigorated, energized, tingling, and ready to enjoy a long, languid soak in the bath.

Try both the following friction treatments. They are based on traditional Scandinavian techniques to cleanse, warm, and tone the body. Although they are stimulating, they don't have to be used only when you want to wake up. An all-over rub will loosen tense muscles and if you follow with a warm, relaxing bath, the final effect will be calming and soothing rather than energizing. They are particularly good after a hard exercise workout, to shift lactic acid before winding down for a bath or massage.

Alternatively, they may be used alone, early in the morning before you shower, to boost energy levels and put a spring in your step for the day's work ahead.

Using cold water after soaking in hot is very invigorating and energizing. It is also a shock to the system and has been known to reduce grown men to tears. Throwing cold water over your partner is not recommended, as it could end a beautiful relationship, but there are more comforting ways of going about it. The combination of hot and cold first dilates, then constricts capillaries near the skin's surface, so that freshly oxygenated blood floods the tissue. It brings nutrients to growing cells, cleanses the backlog of wastes and toxins, and leaves you feeling wide awake and raring to go.

If you are very brave, you can turn off the hot water for the last 30 seconds of a shower and gasp with the shock of it all. But this leaves the body so cold that you'll be covered in goosebumps and shaking while you dry off. It might also be quite dangerous for anyone with circulatory disorders. It is much better to add cold water sparingly so that the body can acclimatize.

Here are the two best methods of taking the unpleasant chill out of cool water bathing: use them whenever you or your partner need to feel revived, refreshed, and energized. As they don't involve a shock to the system, they are perfectly safe for anyone suffering from circulatory

Water is the best cleanser we have and helps remove wastes or grime inside the body and from the skin's surface, with equal speed and efficiency.

deficiencies or heart problems, but check beforehand with your doctor to be absolutely sure.

THE DRY BODY BRUSH

For this you will need a soft, natural-bristle body brush. Nylon brushes, loofahs, and abrasive bath mitts are too rough and tend to scratch skin, leaving it raw or red. Use the brush to rub your partner's body from toe-to-top, without water so there is more friction between bristle and skin. You may add a single drop of an essential oil to the brush to make it more 'scentual'. As your partner needs to stand naked while you brush, it is best to start after you've run the bath so the room is warm; otherwise wind towels around the half of the body you're not working on. Always brush in an upward direction using soft, fast sweeps. To gauge the force required, watch your partner's face. If there is a frown or wince, it is too hard and is hurting; if there's a hint of a smile, it's too light and tickly.

Start on the sole of one foot, then the toes, top of the foot, ankle, and all the way up both sides of the leg to the buttocks. Do the other leg before moving on to the arms, brushing from fingertips to the shoulder. Then start on the torso: first move across the shoulder tops and up the neck, sweep lightly across the chest avoiding the breasts or nipples as they are sensitive. Make large, circular movements around the abdomen, and small circles from the buttock up to the top of the hip, down around the thigh and back up again, then sweep upwards around the waistline. Finally brush the entire back from the thighs up to the shoulders. Pay particular attention to any rough, dry areas of skin, such as on the soles of the feet, knees, or elbows, and to fleshy areas, such as the buttocks or upper arms. Don't brush the face, any skin that is sensitive, healing or marked by a rash, or directly over any moles anywhere on the body.

One friction rub every ten days is enough to keep skin healthy and glowing, but the thicker-skinned can benefit from more frequent brushing. Once you have finished, your partner can jump straight in the bath or shower. It is a good idea to wash the brush immediately with mild soap or detergent to clean it of the skin debris it has collected. Then the natural bristles will have time to dry and stiffen before you need them again.

THE SALT RUB

For this you will need a soft, clean wash cloth and about four ounces of unrefined, coarse sea salt. Start by running a bath so the room is warm. Get your partner to undress, then stand on a bath mat (to prevent the floor from getting messy), dip the wash cloth in the bath water and use it to wet down the body. Squeeze excess water out of the cloth and dip it in a saucer of sea salt, then rub your partner's skin using the salt crystals for friction. Dip the cloth in again regularly as you work from toes-to-top, as in the dry body brush (see above). Avoid the face, genitals or any skin that is scratched, cut, or otherwise injured, as salt tends to sting open wounds. Once you've finished, your partner can step straight into the bath to rinse (shake any salt off the bath mat into the water at the same time) and soak for 15 minutes. You can use the salt rub and bath once a week at the most.

Not only is coarse sea salt granular enough to be abrasive, but it is rich in minerals that are vital for good health, it softens skin, takes the ache out of muscles, and relaxes the body. These minerals nourish all life in the ocean: seaweeds, for instance, contain ten to 20 times as much calcium, iron, potassium, magnesium, iodine, and trace elements as land vegetables. Thalassotherapy, which is a range of spa treatments all using ocean ingredients (sea water, sea salt, algae, plankton, kelp, mud, etc), is based on the belief that when they are heated to body temperature, we can absorb these minerals by osmosis through our skin, and from there into the bloodstream. This is thought to be possible because the ingredients of sea water are so similar to those of human blood plasma, so any kind of salt water is capable of remineralizing the body.

Whether or not this is vital to good health, we only have to smell salt water to feel deliciously uplifted in spirits. Soaking in a sea salt bath definitely helps draw out impurities from the skin and aches from the muscles. When it is preceded by a brisk rub, it is doubly relaxing. If you can't find sea salt in your nearest health shop, you can use coarse Epsom salts or table salt instead. Any saline solution has the bonus of making water more buoyant, so the body floats more freely and escapes the drag of gravity. You may use up to half a pound (240gm) of salt in a bath without irritation, unless you have any cuts, scratches, allergies or extra sensitive skin. But don't use salty water on your face as it can make your eyes sting.

THE SPONGE LUNGE

After a good soak in a warm tub, get your partner to stand up in the bath so his skin begins to cool. Place a natural sea sponge in a basin of cold water until it is soft and swollen, then squeeze it until it is almost dry. Use the damp sponge to massage all over his body from the neck down, until you end up at bath water level. Then dip the sponge in the warm bath and squeeze the water over his shoulders and back several times. Repeat, this time with cold water from the basin squeezed over his back before sponging all over the body. Then pull out the plug and while the bath drains away, use one dip of hot followed by one of cold. Finish by dipping the sponge in cold water, squeezing it until it is almost dry, and rubbing it all over his body so he is cool and refreshed. Then help him

dry off with a brisk towel massage, working from his legs up to his neck.

COLD COMFORT

After soaking for ten minutes in a warm to hot bath, let half the water run out, turn on the cold water and let the bath gradually refill. Lie with your feet under the running water so that the blood vessels constrict, and slowly swirl the bath water with your hands so the hot and cold water mix. As you lie there you will get ripples of cool and warm water all over your body; you really can feel the two temperatures separately for several minutes. When the bath is full again, you will be refreshed, revitalized, and cool, but not shivering. When you get out, keep warm with lots of towels draped all round you. This is an excellent pick-me-up if you come home tired and want to go out an hour later full of energy, especially if you rest after your bath. Once you've dried yourself off (or your partner has, by giving you a brisk all-over rub), lie on the bed wrapped in towels and relax totally.

TOWEL MASSAGE

Dry your partner after any of these toning treatments with a brisk towel massage. Wrap his body in a warm dry towel while you use another to rub his legs dry, from ankles up to the buttocks. Dry his hands and arms in the same way, rubbing firmly but not hard enough to make his skin red and uncomfortable. Rub upwards from the hands to the shoulders. Finally dry his body by draping a long towel around his back and, holding the ends with your hands in front, vigorously pulling it from side to side. Pat any remaining, delicate areas (underarms, chest etc.) gently dry.

Soft soaping your partner

Even the chores of bathtime can be made more enjoyable if a little special pampering is thrown in. One of life's greatest pleasures is having someone else shampoo your hair for you. And if someone else washes your back, it is soothing, sensual, and deep cleanses all those hard to reach patches.

To make it relaxing as well as pleasurable, use the following massage techniques. They combine pressure in just the right spot (to trigger muscle loosening), plenty of rubbing (to stimulate the circulation), and a sensual touch (to pamper totally). Both of you should practise them until they are automatic, and spoil one another by using them often.

THE HAIR RAISING TREAT

There is a correct way to shampoo hair. Most people scrub and tangle their crowning glory rather than wash it. Since it is a growing thing and not a mop, it doesn't take kindly to mistreatment, so from now on, be gentle. You should always shampoo in running water to rinse off all dirt, so you need a shower or spray attachment. The best position is with your partner's head down, to relax the scalp and help blood flow to her head.

First wet the hair thoroughly, then gently rub a blob of shampoo in the palms of your hands and stroke it on the hair from the roots to the ends. Put a little extra shampoo on your fingertips, then massage gently from the hairline up to the crown, all over. Next, place your fingertips back at the hairline, push down, and make tiny circles so that the scalp, rather than your fingers, rotates. Repeat all over the head. Squeeze the suds from the roots to the hair ends, then take hold of sections of hair near the roots and gently tug them to relax the scalp further. Massage all over once more, using your fingertips only. Then with your thumbs at the base of the skull in the centre of the neck, make a series of firm presses out towards the ears. Placing your

hands firmly on either side of the head, push in and hold for a count of five, then repeat all over the skull. Finally, wash all the shampoo out under running water and tap the head all over with your fingertips for a minute before drying it with a towel.

Now your partner's head will be tingling all over and her hair will be glossy and clean. This technique is particularly relaxing and will massage away headaches, stress, and tension, as well as grease and grime.

THE TOTAL BACK TONIC

To wash away aches and pains as you wash a back, you need a lot of suds so that your hands move freely. Start by lathering up with a bar of soap, making circles all over the skin. Then with palms down, squeeze and hold (for a count of five) the muscles all along the shoulders from the neck out on both sides. Do the same to the loose flesh between the shoulder blade and the armpit, and around the waist. Lightly tap the back all over with loosely clenched fists, then rub it up and down with the palms of your hands (for maximum friction, make one hand go up as the other comes down to stretch the skin). Using your thumbs only, make small circles on either side of the spine from the bottom up to the neck, then all around the shoulder blades. Finally, push down gently on the top of the shoulders, then push them forward and pull them back towards you.

You may add any other strokes from the basic back massage (see page 38) if you are in the mood, but end with the gentle shoulder stretches. Rinse your partner's back thoroughly with warm water.

Your partner can wash away aches and pain as she washes your back, using soap suds with a simple massage technique.

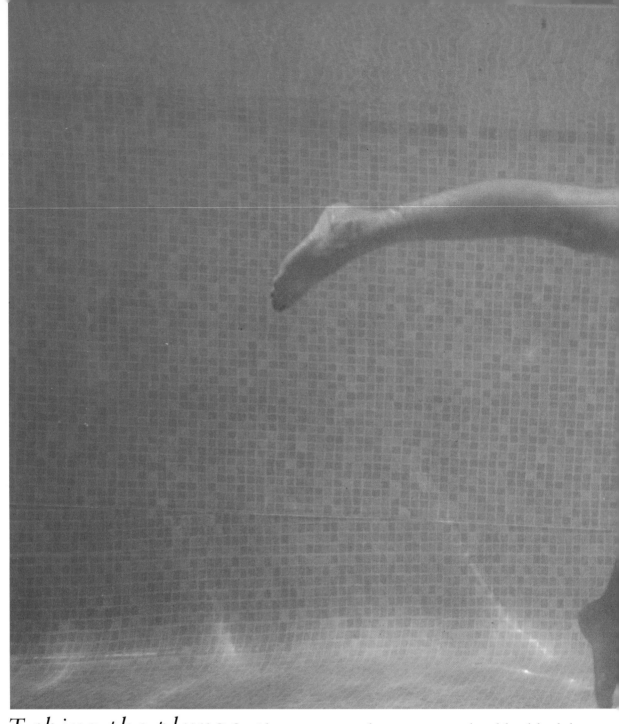

Taking the plunge Almost everyone has access to a local health club or community swimming pool (many offer childminding facilities), so you and your partner can splash out together even if you don't own a backyard pool. Moving through water relaxes and rebuilds muscles, and reduces body weight by up to 90 percent, and this freedom is far more sensual than most other exercise activities.

The gentle surge of water washing against skin instantly puts you in the mood for fun. Half an hour spent swimming burns off more calories than a single game of squash, with far less risk of injury. It is excellent for general mobility, co-ordination, strength, and the heart and lungs. The overarm crawl is the most energetic stroke (200 calories per half hour), followed by butterfly, backstroke, and breaststroke (150 calories per half

hour). Ten to 15 minutes' continuous swimming gives a fairly good workout, but if you are very fit, aim to swim for 15 to 30 minutes.

However, basic lapping can become monotonous and make swimming more of a chore than a pleasure. If you combine your plunge with a workout, both you and your partner can incorporate some specific exercises to trim and tone the problem areas of your bodies: tighten a

Working out in water feels effortless because the body is buoyant, but it tightens and tones muscles effectively since you exercise against the water's resistance.

107

saggy tummy, slim the waist, firm legs, thighs, and buttocks, and strengthen the arms and chest. And since you 'escape' from gravity in water, many exercises that would exhaust you at the gym feel almost effortless in the pool. At the same time, they are often more effective than they would be on solid ground, as you are working out against the water's resistance. Here is a simple exercise routine for you to try: it takes half an hour (five-minute warm up, 20-minute workout, five-minute cool down), but you may just pick out a couple of specific steps to tone problem areas. If you do it from start to finish and still want to swim some laps, do them after step seven but before step eight, when muscles are fully warmed and stretched.

The water works

When you exercise in the pool, you don't need your partner to provide resistance – the water does it for you. Consequently, you can both work through the following exercise routines at the same time, offering each other advice and encouragement.

WARM UP: Jump up and down in chest deep water for two minutes, moving from one leg to the other and going backwards and forwards in hops. Walk across the width of the pool for three minutes, using big strides as quickly as you can.

ARM TONER: Stand in water deep enough to cover your shoulders, with your feet apart and your arms at your sides. Bend one arm and raise it so the palm is in front (and facing) the chest. Straighten the elbow and push the arm out to the side at shoulder height. Relax and repeat ten times with each arm.

CHEST/ARM STRENGTHENER: Stand in chest deep water, bend forward and using your arms only, do the breaststroke for two minutes, then the overarm crawl for two minutes – without moving forward, and keeping feet flat on the pool bottom for balance.

LEG/THIGH TRIMMER: Stand in chest deep water, side on to the edge of the pool, with one hand holding the wall for balance and the other straight out to the side at shoulder height. Swing the outside leg up

You can adapt the arm toner exercise by working both arms at once. This helps to strengthen the muscles in the upper arm, chest, and back.

high in front, then back as far as possible, keeping it straight in a long, slow stretch. Repeat ten times, then turn around and repeat with the other leg.

TUMMY TIGHTENER: Lie on your back with your head towards the pool wall and, with outstretched arms, hold onto a ladder, rail, wall, or ledge at head height. Bend your knees and slowly bring them up towards your chest, using your abdominal muscles. Hold for a count of ten, then relax and straighten legs out again. Repeat 15 times.

WAIST WHITTLER: At the deepest end of the pool, face the wall and hold onto the edge or a rail with your elbows bent. Keeping legs together and toes pointed, swing from the waist, first to one side, then the other, like a pendulum. Repeat ten times each side.

LEG/BOTTOM TIGHTENER: At the deep end of the pool, hold onto the side and stretch out face down with your face above the water. Keeping legs straight, kick rapidly for two minutes. Rest, then repeat. In the same position, do the frog kick (by bending knees, widening legs, straightening, and pulling together) for two minutes. If you wish, you may now swim several lengths of the pool.

COOL DOWN: Repeat the warm up exercises (see the first step, above) for five minutes.

The bath plugger

To make any of the bathtime treatments more effective, try a short series of tub exercises while you soak. Not only will they help you relax, by gently stretching and releasing muscle tension, but they will also tone your body and increase suppleness and flexibility. Do them after you have soothed muscles with an aromatherapy soak, a dry body brush, a salt rub, or even the total back tonic

technique. At least they will guarantee that you are gainfully employed as you bask in the bath. Including a mini workout will make you feel less guilty about staying in the tub so long and deserting your unpampered partner.

Don't be carried away with enthusiasm. If you are too energetic, you might slip and injure yourself.

LEG/LOWER BACK STRETCH: Lying as flat as possible in the bath, without submerging, raise one leg and bend the knee so your calf is parallel with the water. Straighten your leg up in the air, point your toes, and hold the stretch for a count of eight. Then draw the knee down to your chest by bending it and holding it around the calf for a count of eight. Relax, and lower the leg back into the water. Repeat ten times on each leg.

SPINE/TORSO STRETCH: Sitting down, bend forwards, stretching your hands along your legs and holding them as near to the feet as possible. Hold position for a count of ten. Relax and straighten up slowly, then repeat six times.

ARM/CHEST/SHOULDER STRETCH: Holding a soapy sponge, raise your hand above your head, bend the elbow, and lower the sponge down to the middle of your shoulders. Make large circles on your back, five clockwise with the right hand, before changing to the left hand and making five counterclockwise circles. Repeat the entire exercise with each hand once more.

WAIST/ABDOMINAL STRETCH: Sitting up in the bath with a straight back, turn from the waist and place your left hand on the outside of your right knee. At the same time, slip your right hand behind your back and grasp your left arm above the elbow. Hold for a count of ten, then repeat four times on each side (place your right hand on your left knee and your left hand behind your back to stretch your other side.).

Time *for* together*ness* is vital for a happy, healthy life. The average human body is sustained physically by 2,000–3,000 calories, 23,000 gulps of air, up to eight hours' sleep, and 3–5 pints of water every day. But our emotional needs are impossible to quantify. All we know for sure is that the body and mind are inseparable, and both need nurturing before they can function as a whole.

The better we feel personally, the better we perform publicly – so that we rise to life's challenges rather than being swamped by them. As our daily lives become more complex, it is the mind that takes the pressure, long before the body shows any physical signs of wear and tear. And since research now proves that the human brain can energize and activate bodily functions – just as a motor runs a machine – it is vital to take time out to refuel mentally, as well as physically.

The psyche, ego, Self, spirit, or whatever else you choose to call it, needs constant tender loving care. It comes from within, but is shaped and strengthened from without. We are restored mentally and emotionally by the attentions of those closest to us – and we grow closer to them at the same time. Just as the mating instinct leads animals to the safety of their lair, the bonds we form with a partner provide an intimate sanctuary from a tough, hard world. But it is a sanctuary that we have less and less time to retreat to, or to enjoy once we get there.

We stagger home late at night and automatically respond to our obvious bodily needs: a quick meal to quiet the pangs of hunger, a television screen to blank out mental turmoil, and sleep to give us the physical strength to face the following day. Our deeper, emotional needs don't have an early warning system, and limp along until they collapse under pressure. Then they surface in the form of constant arguments, unhappiness, an illness, depression, or as a general crisis. Unless we make time regularly to restore the motor, the machine eventually stops.

This is why it is so important to take time out to relax together, at least once a week. Even a brief escape will recharge and revitalize energy levels. Not only does it make every relationship healthier, but it also heals the mind and body in a way that nothing else can. It restores the part of the psyche that Freud called the id – the unconscious, instinctual, primitive side of the personality, as opposed to the external ego which we reveal to the outside world.

While everyone around us sees a strong, confident, competent human being, only our partner can spoil, pamper, and adore the whims of the child within. And being able to laugh at our foibles, share our worries, flop in a heap, and find the funny side of fear or failure with someone who cares, lightens the load instantly.

Although making time to be alone together sounds like a cliché, it is the most valuable way of using the brief spells of leisure left over from an action-packed life. Most of us blurt out problems – from a bill that came through the mail to a bitch about the office – while rushing around the home and catching up on the chores. We talk above the noise of the food processor, the clanging of saucepans, the television set, or the other sounds of daily life, and hear without really listening. And although this unburdens the brain, it does nothing to relax the body or release deeper emotions. The only way to share them is by having 15 minutes every night, or an hour once a week, when together you escape totally. How you use the time is as personal as your own relationship. From a walk around the garden to an intimate, specially planned weekly meal – with candles, soothing music and the chance to taste the food (rather than bolt it) and laugh or talk (rather than just chew). Even something as simple as refuelling the body with calories can become more pleasurable if you use it as time to relax together. And good food and wine can delight the senses in the most frivolous way. Think of Shrove Tuesday without the pancakes, or Thanksgiving minus the turkey; fun and feasting go hand in hand.

There are many different levels of relaxation, but some of the ways we think we relax aren't really beneficial at all. Entertainment may be enjoyable, but going out to dinner or going to the movies doesn't necessarily lessen nervous energy or reduce the body's stress hormones. And a frantic bout of exercise can release pent-up anger and worry from the mind in a cathartic way, but once you get over the exhaustion, the worries return and the muscles are often tenser due to lactic acid build-up. The deepest levels of relaxation come from letting go completely. Even just lying down together on the floor and giving in to gravity can make the muscles and mind go limp. The best position is semi-supine, which aligns the spine, loosens the lower back and encourages total indolence. You need to lie face up on the floor with your head resting on some books (try two telephone directories) and feet flat to the floor, with knees bent. Then concentrate on sinking into the ground until your whole body feels heavy and floppy. After ten minutes, even the mind and tongue loosen up, so it is a pleasant way to catch up and chat about the day.

There are many relaxing techniques that really do reach the deeper levels of the psyche: yoga, meditation, chanting, hypnosis, creative visualization, and biofeedback, for instance. But they all involve learning, practice, perseverance, and putting aside the time to perform them, which is an effort in itself. And as they are personal experiences, rather than shared ones, they should be employed outside the time you put aside for togetherness. There are simpler ways of getting in touch with your partner's needs, just by listening to them. But first, it is important to understand what you are up against – and how you can easily change some areas of your lifestyle to lessen the entire load.

The stress factor

Despite its reputation, stress itself is neither bad nor good. It has become the dirty word of the decade, but without it we wouldn't rise to a challenge, pursue dreams or ambitions, strive quite so hard, or function so creatively. In fact, it is how we respond to pressure that determines how it affects us – and that can be either negatively or positively.

When mind and body are in the firing line, mental tension translates automatically into physical symptoms, via the sympathetic autonomic nervous system, which is affiliated to the stimulating hormones, like adrenalin. A small dose of pressure gives tiny physical changes such as butterflies in the tummy as a result of increased secretions of digestive enzymes, or an ashen, pallid face, when surface blood vessels constrict. These are just signs of the body tensing itself to take action; if it didn't, you wouldn't have the spurt of energy to run across the road and escape an oncoming truck. But if you are facing a long, heavy task, rather than a heavy goods vehicle, the tension mounts without physical release. Eventually it surfaces with headaches, muscle pains, sleeplessness, grumpiness, loss of appetite, loss of libido, dizzy spells, nausea, panic attacks, high blood pressure, or an irregular heart rate. Continual, constant stress triggers dozens of diseases or even leads to total physical collapse.

Research confirms the role of stress as a contributing factor to almost everything that ails modern man. However, doctors also now know that stress appears not as the result of a particular event, but as the symptom of how we choose to perceive that event. This link between mind, body, and well-being is taking modern medicine in a new direction in the next decade. Although we cannot always control what happens in life, we do have considerable say over how we let it affect us. It is only recently that researchers have been able to prove that we can control the stress trigger, or sympathetic autonomic nervous system. We can also activate its opposite – the parasympathetic system of nerves, which are affiliated to the calming, resting hormones. Clinical studies show that we can alter automatic body functions – slow a pounding heart or lower blood pressure, for instance – just by thinking about it. And the miraculous way that we manage this, is simply by taking time out consciously to relax.

The power of the human mind is immeasurable. Using it consciously to relax at the end of a frantic day is the single

most effective antidote to stress. But while you are actually working, you can use brain-power for a temporary respite that is nearly as effective. If we learn how to channel the energy burst supplied by the sympathetic system, stress can be used positively the instant it strikes. When faced with inhuman demands – whether its a long shopping list or a huge stack of paperwork – we invariably think 'I can't do it, it's too much, it's impossible, HELP'.

This is the negative panic point, when stress rears its ugly head. By thinking positively, you can use the adrenalin burst to look at what you *can* do. The most important tasks take priority, you don't panic, and you use the energy actively to do the job quicker anyway. In addition, if we control the stress caused by simple things, it is less likely to build up to bursting point in the long term.

Using your mind to make your body

relax only works if you make yourself think about it. So by setting time aside each week not only to unwind, but also to be alone with your partner, you are consciously creating the switch-off situation. And once you mentally switch off the pressure, you can start sharing the more positive side of your relationship. Soaking in a hot bath or enjoying a massage switches off the pressure automatically – as explained in previous chapters – by working from the outside of the body and reaching in to the deeper levels of the psyche. But conscious relaxation is an added bonus, that starts within and works outwards. It is not something that just happens, but if you manage to master it, every aspect of your lives will be healthier. And each of the pampering plans in this book contributes by drawing you closer to your partner and closer to the pleasures of life.

Setting time aside each week to be alone with your partner helps you escape from the pressure of the world, and helps you build a more intimate, positive relationship together.

Close encounters of the absurd kind

Tickle therapy might sound like a joke, but it can be seriously good for you. Laughter is the shortest distance between two people; it not only increases rapport and intimacy, but also makes you feel happy, positive, and lighthearted. It affects the body almost as much as the mind. A giggling fit makes you gasp for air, makes the heart pound, the blood pressure rise, and sends fresh oxygen and nutrients surging through the arteries. It also makes your muscles floppy and weak, to the extent that if you are carrying anything when someone cracks a joke, you tend to let go. This release-effect continues long after the smile fades. Once the blood pressure drops, the heart slows again, and the muscles regain control, you are calm, euphoric, and deeply relaxed.

Research now shows that this is because laughter uses up some of the body's stress hormones, like adrenalin, which is burned off by any burst of energy. But tickling the funny bone goes much deeper than just beating stress. It wipes away anger, frustration, anxiety, and many other negative emotions. It makes you feel closer to anyone who laughs with you, just by sharing something intimate and frivolous together. It puts things in perspective, and puts you in a good mood.

There is more and more scientific evidence that being in a good mood benefits all areas of our overall health and well-being. Psychoneuroimmunology, or the study of how the mind affects the health, is so new that its importance can not yet be gauged, but its future possibilities seem to be unlimited. It seems the human brain is not only capable of triggering the body's immune system, but also has the power to boost it. And just as negative thoughts of anxiety, stress, and depression can make us ill, positive thoughts of happiness, hope, and feeling loved can make us healthy. This has been proved in hundreds of studies worldwide. On the simplest level, mind power has stopped test groups catching a common

cold; on a deeper level, a positive mental approach has been shown to increase the chances of recovering from a disease as serious as cancer, by slowing the progression of malignancy.

Although one day we might be able to think ourselves healthy, in the meantime laughter is still the best medicine we have close to hand. And you don't have to do a star turn every night as a stand-up comic to make it effective. It isn't about inventing a sense of humour, but about finding yours. By seeing the funny side of life and sharing it with your partner, you are actually escaping into a private world and enjoying it together. It is simply a way of stressing the positive, rather than dwelling on the negative. When you lighten up your mood, you lighten the load of life's pressures. Even if you can't find anything genuinely funny to laugh about, you can still use the comedian's basic technique: take a step back, look from a different perspective, take aim, and kick the world in the seat of its pants.

A private joke at the world's expense is one thing, but humour is now taken so seriously that it has gone public on a global scale. Today's top executives from some of the largest multinational corporations are made to attend seminars where they try to learn to be funny. Not only does this help corporate communications, but it has also been shown to increase sales and production, improve a company's public image, cut medical costs, and make employees stay with a company longer because they enjoy working there. The very fact that big businesses are prepared to spend millions just to raise a laugh, means there must be something in it. Politicians have proved this theory time and time again, by using a witty speech to win votes. The same principle works in the privacy of your own home—we love to laugh, but we love the people who make us laugh even more. Learning to share the funny side of life with your partner strengthens the bonds between you by

Learning to share the funny side of life draws you closer and lets you share a private joke at the world's expense.

making you closer, happier, and more loving. You become intimate allies together, and a united force against the stresses of the world.

Although life would be very dull if it always ran smoothly, we have so many mental and physical demands that when we hit a calm patch, we collapse into it rather than being buoyed up by it. Our bodies are so overloaded with pressure that they fuse long before we pull out the plug and switch off. Learning to get the balance of power right, between the opposite forces of stress and relaxation, is the key that takes the pressure off. And using the mind to see the flip side of problems and cope with them positively makes life less troublesome.

The flip side of stress

It is said that 200,000 frowns make one permanent wrinkle. That is a lot of internal worry before the first sign shows. The more chance you get to defuse worries along the way, the less of them there are in life. Taking time out to be together is the first step. The second way of taking positive action is to break the routine of all work and all play. Deep relaxation comes from letting go and enjoying a moment of calm, serene stillness. This is what puts the balance of power on an even keel before you burn yourself out. Anyone who suffers from stress knows that it is addictive.

The stress addict looks at life as an egg-and-spoon race. They constantly juggle demands, deadlines, daily routines, dates, and dinner engagements, and are always rushing like mad to catch up. They bolt meals, stitch up business deals, gulp bottles of wine, hurry conversations without listening, drive for a weekend 'break' through ten towns in two days, and even make love like a dash to the finish line. They don't stop, because if they did, they would never get started again.

Taking control of a busy life is simple. You just have to make a conscious

decision to take time off to recharge. And no matter what else is happening in your lives, you make this time sacrosanct. You spend it together, alone. And you make it as beneficial as possible, mentally and physically.

If your lives really are action-packed, you won't be able to reach a deeper state of relaxation without first pulling the plug on the power source. There are many quick tricks to switch off, and it is vital to use them to get out of overdrive before moving into neutral. Otherwise you can pummel your partner without really pampering him, soothe the body with warm water while the brain is still at boiling point, and leave the senses and the emotions well alone, even when you are both close together. The relaxing techniques described here are designed to be used to prepare the mind and body for the pleasures in the rest of the book. They take no more than 15 minutes of your valuable time, but instantly put you in the right mood for anything else – whether it is just enjoying a brief spell of solitude together, or two hours of top-to-toe spoiling and self-indulgence.

Tension tends to build up in awkward, unreachable areas like the nape of the neck, between the shoulders and low in the back. So the following three routines need a combined effort to be totally beneficial. If your partner performs the stretches on your relaxed body, they're not only more effective, but more pleasurable. Take turns to be the one who does the work.

Each exercise should be done slowly, gradually and gently: never force tired muscles into a new position or you might damage them. The point is not to pull muscles, but to stretch and extend them gently, hold the position for anything up to 30 seconds, then softly release them so the tension melts away. If your partner is stronger than you, be extra cautious or they'll turn into a tug-of-war rather than a show of love. The routines are even more relaxing if you listen to music but choose something soothing. You can't do slow movements to a disco beat!

Time for togetherness

Six high-pressure points

This routine is ideal for great thinkers. It releases mental tension instantly, as well as loosening the muscles that automatically knot when you spend your days sitting at a desk and bending over work. It involves a series of body presses, rather than exercises, which relax the shoulders, neck, scalp, head and upper back, and chest. Your partner should sit comfortably on a chair with a low back to support her waist, while you stand and deliver. Make sure she keeps an upright position, so that her spine and head are in a line. Do the individual presses from start to finish, before repeating any.

Place your left hand, palm down, against her forehead and your right hand across the nape of her neck, so that your thumb and fingers are outstretched, almost from ear to ear. The exact position of the right hand, should follow the occiput (or skull) bone. The simplest way to find it, is by running your finger up the nape of her neck over the spinal column to the natural hollow at the top – the occiput runs in a horizontal line from that point, around the head towards the ears. Check that your

2

partner's head is straight up to avoid bending her neck, then gently press both your hands inwards, hold for a count of 20, then relax the pressure. This releases tension in the entire head.

Using your right hand only, place it in exactly the same position with your palm against her forehead. Then gently press down – *not* backwards or forwards – as if pushing the head into the shoulders. Hold for a count of ten, then relax. This loosens the scalp and relaxes the temples.

1. With your left hand against her forehead and the right supporting the skull bone, press both hands inwards for a count of 20.

2. Press down with your hand on her forehead for a count of ten, then relax.

3. With your hand supporting the skull bone at the nape of the neck, squeeze inwards for a count of ten.

4. Press down into both shoulder muscles for a count of 20, then relax.

With your right hand in the same position as in step one (supporting the occiput bone), get your partner to relax her neck by bending it forward until she is comfortable. Then gently pinch your fingers together so you are pressing by squeezing your hand inwards (*not* pushing downwards), hold for a count of ten, then relax. This removes tension at the base of the skull and stretches the neck.

Place each hand on one of her shoulders, over the large muscles which run from the neck out to the arm/collarbone joint. Your thumbs should be on her back, with your fingers pointing down towards her chest. Make sure she is sitting upright and not slumped forward. Gently press down into her body, hold for a count of 20, then relax. This stretches the neck and shoulders simultaneously.

Place both hands palm down around the top of each of her arms, just below the outer shoulders. Make sure she is sitting upright, then gently press her shoulders forward, in other words, *in* towards her chest, hold for a count of 20, and then relax. This stretches the upper back muscles and the shoulder muscles on either side of the neck.

With your hands in exactly the same position as the previous step, gently pull her shoulders back towards you, hold for a count of 20, and relax. This stretches the upper chest area and loosens the muscles that support the shoulder blades.

Make sure your partner sits with a straight spine throughout. Repeat any presses that she particularly needs once the sequence is complete.

5

5. Holding the top of her arms, press her shoulders forward and hold for a count of 20, then relax.

6. Holding the top of her arms, gently pull her shoulders back for a count of 20.

6

2

Six power pushes

1. Let her straighten her legs and push against the weight of your chest for a count of 15. Keep your knees bent to avoid strain.

2. While she tries to straighten her leg and push upwards, add a gentle downward resistance for a count of ten.

This routine releases the energy from built-up stress in a more positive way, so you can use it afterwards. It is invigorating, so is ideal for times when you're feeling tired and tense but need to wake up your sluggish system. Use it half way through a task, to give you the spurt to complete it, or when you're tired and need to be re-energized for whatever comes next in the evening. Basically, your partner acts as a weight machine and adds the resistance to the stretches you are trying to perform. So you need more effort to do them, and the trapped lactic acid in muscles or excess adrenalin in the body is triggered for action.

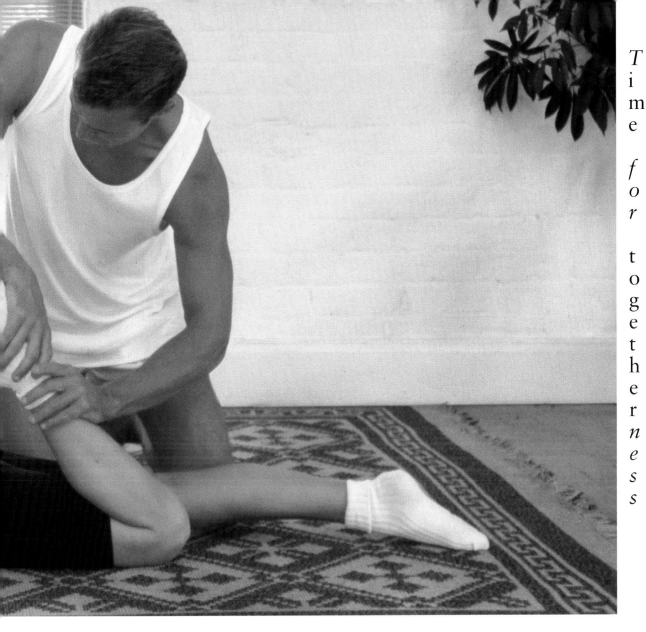

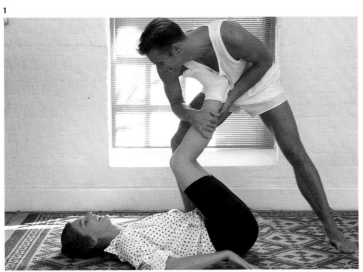

1

Your partner should lie on her back, with her legs raised upwards and her knees bent, while you stand beside her and lower your chest against her feet. Let her straighten her legs and push into your lower chest for count of 15, while you add resistance by gently leaning down, and then relax back into the start position. This works the thigh and buttock muscles.

Get your partner to turn over and lie face down on the floor, with legs straight. Kneel by her side and, holding one foot at the ankle, bend her leg up towards her bottom. While she tries to push up and straighten her leg, add gentle resistance by lightly pressing downwards for a count of 10, then relax. Repeat on the other leg.

3

This works the upper thighs and the hamstrings behind the knees.

Your partner should lie on her side, with her top leg straight and the lower one bent, with the knee slightly forward. Stand beside her, holding her top leg near the ankle, and as she tries to raise the leg upwards, add downwards resistance with the weight of your arms for a count of 10. Turn over to work the other leg. This exercises the outer thigh and hip muscles.

With your partner sitting upright in a chair, kneel on the floor and face her. Get her to stretch her hands out to the side at shoulder level, then bend them upwards from the elbows, with palms facing towards the sides of her head. Place your hands on the inside of her forearms, and as she tries to bring her elbows towards the middle of her chest, add gentle resistance outwards for a count of 15, then relax. This works the pectoral muscles.

Stand facing one another, with enough

3. As she tries to raise her top leg, add gentle resistance with the weight of your arms for a count of 10.

4. As she tries to bring her bent elbows towards the middle of her chest, add gentle resistance by pushing outwards for a count of 15, then relax.

4

5

5. While she moves her arms out to the sides at shoulder height, add resistance for a count of 15 by gently holding her wrists.

6. Pull her knees towards you to keep her feet flat on the floor, while she curls her shoulders forwards for a count of 15.

6

space between you for your partner to have her arms straight out in front, elbows slightly bent, with palms facing inwards. Hold the outer arms, near her wrists, and add resistance for a count of 15, while she moves her hands out to the sides of her body at shoulder level, then relax. This works the shoulder muscles.

Sit on the floor facing your partner, while she lies face upwards – both of you should have your knees bent at a 45° angle. You provide resistance throughout by pulling your partner's knees toward you and keeping her feet flat to the floor. She should place her hands on her thighs and stretch them up to her knees, as she curls her shoulders upwards (keeping her chin tucked into her chest throughout). Then hold this position as a curl for a count of 15, before you both relax. Repeat again twice more, keeping the whole movement slow and fluid. This works the abdominal muscles and strengthens the tummy.

Six tension busters This routine will stretch and release trapped tension, and instantly leaves you feeling floppy and calm. It is ideal for floor-pacers, or anyone who is so wound up that he can't sit still, let alone relax. It works through all the major muscle groups from top-to-toe, so it is important to do the stretches in the order they are shown. You need to wear loose, comfortable clothing and have a bit of clear floor space before you start. Do each stretch slowly and gently, concentrating on keeping the correct position throughout. Since men are often more muscular and less supple than women, you'll probably find a big difference in flexibility.

Get your partner to sit on the floor with his knees bent, his back as straight as possible, and his arms above his head. You need to stand behind him, side on, so that your right leg is touching and supporting the length of his back. Then slip your arms through his and firmly hold his biceps. Gently stretch his arms behind him, by pulling back, hold for a count of 20, and relax. This stretches the chest and opens it out, while relaxing the muscles around the shoulder blades.

Sit on the floor facing one another, with your backs straight. Keep your legs flat to the ground, with his feet inside yours, so that your legs are wider apart (this allows for the height difference, if he is taller than you). Hold one another around the wrists, and then using the weight of your upper body, gradually lean back so that you stretch his body forwards. Hold for a count of 30, and relax by letting him pull you both to an upright sitting position. Only your torsos should move throughout – if your legs do, then you are trying to 'see-saw' rather than gently stretch. This exercise extends the upper back and shoulders so they relax totally.

1. Support the length of his back against your leg and gently stretch his arms behind him for a count of 20, then relax.

2. Stretch his upper back and shoulders by pulling his torso towards you for a count of 30, then relax.

3

palm downward, below his shoulders. You stand on either side of his hips, bend your knees (so you don't strain your back later), and hold him under his arms. While he slightly extends his arms for balance, you gently lift his chest up off the floor towards you, hold for a count of 30, and relax back down. This stretches all the muscles in his lower back, which is one of the main areas where tension builds up, causing discomfort.

While your partner lies face down on the floor and relaxes with his arms by his sides, you kneel beside him, holding one foot around the ankle. Gently bend his leg upwards, pushing his heel towards his bottom, and hold for a count of 20 before relaxing. How far you can take the stretch depends on his flexibility – it may be merely a right angle between the knee and the calf, or right down so his heel touches his buttock. Repeat the complete stretch on the other leg. This actually relaxes the thigh muscles, and does not work the lower leg at all.

Get your partner to turn over, so he is lying on his back, with one leg straight on the floor, and the other bent at the knee. Stand at his feet, facing him and lift his bent leg, leaning forwards so his foot rests

3. To stretch the side of his body, gently pull his raised arm towards you and hold for a count of 25, keeping your backs upright throughout.

4. Gently lift his chest up off the floor for a count of 30, keeping your knees bent throughout.

Sit side by side on the floor, about 18 inches apart, with your knees bent and your backs straight. Each of you should raise your outer arm above your head and hold hands in the middle, with your inner arm bent at the elbow for support. Gently pull his hand towards you to stretch the outer side of his body, hold for a count of 25, and relax. It is important to keep your backs upright throughout, so that he leans towards you, rather than forwards or backwards. You then need to turn around, so you are sitting facing the opposite direction, to repeat the exercise on the other side. This stretches both sides of his torso, from the hip, through the waist, to the arm.

Get your partner to lie face down on the floor, legs together, feet flexed (so his toes are parallel with the ground), and hands

4

on your shoulder. Slowly straighten his leg until it is almost perpendicular, by using your hands to straighten his knee and push it down towards your chest, as you use your shoulder to support the weight of his leg. Once he feels a fairly gentle stretch, hold for a count of 20, then relax. Repeat the stretch on the other leg. This is a basic hamstring exercise designed to relax the muscles along the back of the leg.

5

5. Gently bend his leg back towards his bottom and hold for a count of 20, without pushing down further than is comfortable.

6. Push gently down on his knee as you raise his leg for a count of 20, using your shoulder to support the weight.

6

Playing footsie

Pampering the feet is one of the fastest ways to relax totally and titillatingly. Feet are tough, but respond quickly to a kind touch and spread well-being throughout the body, due to the 72,000 nerves that end up in each sole. Traditional Chinese medicine has always put feet first, believing that the body has lines of energy (or meridians) that end there, which can be stimulated by acupuncture needles. Reflexology, an American adaptation of a similar principle, uses massage and pressure on points only in the feet to benefit the organs in all parts of the body at the receiving end of this tangle of nerves.

If you don't have time for a soothing, sensual foot massage (see page 43), you can still treat your feet by soaking away the day's stresses with a ten minute footbath. The warm water relaxes all the tiny support muscles that help transport the entire body with every step you take. This releases the trapped nerves, so energy flows again from toe-to-top, while also stimulating the circulation. You can make it doubly therapeutic, by switching off the mind at the same time – try listening to music, watching television, or catching up on your reading. It is another way of enjoying a brief spell of stillness in a busy life. And if you use a big bowl, there is room for two, so you and your partner can cuddle up and play footsie in one go.

Make a footbath more sensual by adding extra ingredients. Essential oils stimulate the nose as well as the feet in many different ways (see page 98). A brisk scrub with coarse sea salt (see page 102), followed by a soak, gets rid of dry skin, gives a mini-massage, and soothes away aches and pains. Using hot water, followed by a dip in a second basin of icy-cold, dilates and constricts blood vessels in turn, to invigorate the circulation and the mood. Here are a few recipes for an instant sole nurturing pick-me-up.

FOR A STIMULATING, ENERGIZING SOAK

The best essential oils to revitalize tired feet are cinnamon, eucalyptus, juniper, lemon, peppermint, rosemary, or thyme. Use three drops in total per footbath (approximately 9 pints/5 litres of water). The most pleasing combinations to stimulate the nose at the same time include: one drop each of juniper, lavender, and rosemary; one drop each of cinnamon, lemon, and sandalwood; two drops of eucalyptus with one drop of peppermint; or one drop of lavender with two drops of thyme.

FOR AN AROUSING, SENSUAL SOAK

The essential oils to use that stir the senses and the soles are clary sage, jasmine, neroli, patchouli, rose, sandalwood, or ylang-ylang – in the same quantities as above. For extra potent combinations, try: one drop each of jasmine, neroli, and rose; one drop each of clary sage, sandalwood, and ylang-ylang; two drops of neroli with one drop of rose; or one drop of clary sage with two drops of patchouli.

Some essential oils are particularly good for foot problems. Try Moroccan camomile for itchiness, clary sage for excess perspiration, eucalyptus or lemon for coldness and slow blood circulation, and tea-tree for any fungal infections or to soothe blisters.

Pampering the feet soothes and relaxes the entire body, by triggering the 72,000 nerve endings that lie in the sole of each foot.

Time for togetherness

Digital delights

Feet and hands are the most mobile parts of the body, and to keep them that way, they need regular care and cosseting. But because they do so many tasks automatically – from peeling a grape to piloting us along a busy street – we notice their martyrdom only when something goes wrong with them. Ninety percent of all foot problems are the result of neglect and misuse, and 90 percent of women over 40 only look their age if you judge them by their hands.

A regular, fortnightly manicure and pedicure will help keep hands and feet as fit as the rest of your body, throughout your life. But this need not be a chore. Both hands and feet are richly supplied with nerve endings, and stimulating them is as pleasant as playing with some of the body's more obvious erogenous zones. Holding hands with your partner is intimate and loving, but stroking, petting, and playing with them at the same time is far more sensual. As both hands and feet are supported by tiny interlocking bones and dozens of minute muscles, it is important to rub and relax them – tension from typing, holding a pen, standing all day, or walking in cramped shoes affects the whole body. If you combine this pampering with a preventative manicure or pedicure (*before* you get torn cuticles, ingrown nails, or calluses), hands and feet not only look better, but feel better as well.

Here are the basic steps to the most therapeutic type of manicure and pedicure; they have lots of special touches that a beautician won't think to throw in at a salon appointment. Each takes 15 minutes from start to finish, which is very much quicker than if your partner tried to do it herself. And if you combine them with other treats in the book, they will be even more beneficial: start the pedicure with a relaxing footbath (see page 132), or follow it with the foot massage (see page 43); have a manicure before any massage (see The loving touch) so your hands are

warm, relaxed, and supple, or get your partner to treat your hands after you have given him the salt body rub (see page 102). When giving a pedicure, try the papaya dry skin exfoliator (see page 80) on any rough patches on the feet. The lemon hand cream (see page 78) is excellent for whitening nails and soothing hands as part of the manicure. And since skin needs to be soft and supple for either treatment, soak the hands or feet in warm water mixed with two drops of your favourite essential oil before beginning. For hands: Moroccan camomile calms itchiness, geranium is particularly good for cracked skin, and lavender is soothing and relaxing. For feet: try lemon for slow circulation, tea-tree for soreness or infections, cinnamon for tired arches, clary sage for excessive perspiration, or any of the oils recommended for adding to footbaths (see page 132).

The basic equipment needed is: nail clippers to trim nails, emery boards to file and shape them, orange sticks and cotton balls to push back cuticles and clean under nails, and a piece of chamois leather and buffing paste to shine nails and stimulate circulation. All these are available at drugstores or chemist shops. Always work on one hand or foot at a time, from start to finish, then begin the other.

Always remove varnish from nails before you start. You can apply fresh coats afterwards, if your partner usually wears it (see page 136).

The magical manicure

Soak the hand in a bowl of warm water for five minutes to soften skin and cuticles before starting. Add two drops of an essential oil, or one tablespoon of olive oil (for dry skin), the juice of half a lemon to whiten nails and even out skin tone, or half a cup of fresh pineapple juice to loosen very dry, torn or overgrown cuticles.

Use the tapered end of an orange stick to lift and push back the cuticle around each nail; be gentle at the base, or you'll damage the new nail forming below the skin. Then roll some cotton around the pointed end of the orange stick and run it gently under each nail to clean under the tips.

Trim nails with clippers if necessary; keep them all the same length and give them an oval or slightly squared shape. If you trim them into a point, the sides of the nails will weaken and break with use. File each nail with an emery board so it is smooth. Work from the side to the middle of each nail in half strokes. If you file backwards and forwards you will weaken the nail.

Apply a dab of buffing paste and polish it off using your thumb wrapped in a piece of chamois leather. This adds a long-lasting shine to nails, and works like a mini

1. Use the tapered end of an orange stick gently to lift and push back cuticles.

2. Rub an orange stick wrapped in cotton under each nail to clean the tips.

3. File and shape each nail from the side to the middle in half strokes, using an emery board.

2

3

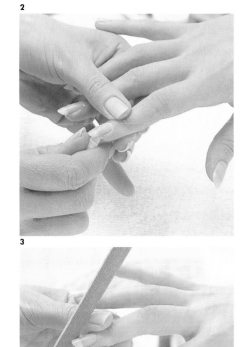

1

massage, bringing blood to the fingertips so nails grow stronger and healthier.

Using lots of massage oil (see The loving touch) or a favourite hand cream, start playing with your partner's hand. The skin here has few sebaceous glands and is often fine and dry. This is one of the reasons hands show signs of age so quickly. The more moisturizer you massage in, the better. Start by stretching the palms out widthways, the fingers backwards and the knuckles downwards, to relax the hand. Then rub it vigorously with friction strokes between your own hands. Gently pull and twist each finger and the thumb from the base to tip. Then using your thumbs only, gently massage in small circles around the wrist. Using your thumbs and fingers, gently knead and fan

4. Rub plenty of massage oil or hand-cream all over the back and palm of the hand.

5. Gently pull and twist each finger from base to tip.

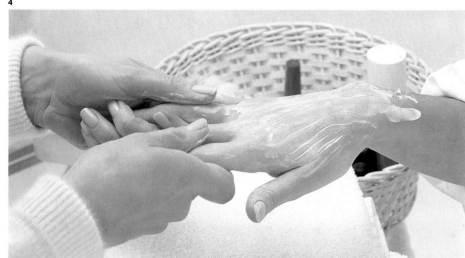

stroke all the tiny bones from fingertips to wrist. Finally, sandwich the hand between your palms at the wrist and pull towards you in a slow, long stroke, ending with the fingertips. Experiment and include any other special touches that your partner particularly likes.

If your partner wears nail polish or varnish, remove any oiliness from her nails by buffing with a cotton pad. Apply a base coat, and when it is dry, paint two thin coats of varnish, allowing them to dry completely between applications. You can apply a top coat to prevent chipping.

The pampering pedicure

Start by soaking the foot in a bowl of warm water for five minutes, to soften skin and cuticles. Add an essential oil or any of the other skin soothers suggested above.

Follow step two of the manicure, but be extra gentle when cleaning under the nails as toenails grow more deeply.

Trim nails with clippers, cutting straight across each toenail; never cut down at the sides or they are likely to become ingrown. File them with an emery board (see step three, manicure).

Buff the toenails in the same way as described in step four of the manicure.

Using lots of massage oil or moisturizer, sandwich the foot between the palms of your hands and stroke firmly from the toes towards the ankles. Vigorously rub the heel with your palms for two minutes to stimulate blood flow and warm the foot. Then hold and wiggle the toes, before gently pulling each one from base to tip. Push under the arch of the foot with your knuckles, and then knead the entire sole, from the ball to heel of the foot. Massage all around the ankle, making small circles with your thumbs. Twist and wring the foot, and finish by sandwiching it between your palms and stroking slowly and firmly from the ankle to the toes several times. Experiment and include your own other special touches.

The air lift

A healthy human body can last weeks without food, days without water, but only minutes without oxygen. Air has always been thought of as our life force: gurus who meditate call it *prana*, the Japanese who practice shiatsu say it is *ki*, and in the Chinese medicine of acupuncture it's named *chi*. This life force provides our energy, which is vital to the chemistry of all living matter – from metabolizing a single skin cell to breaking down a currant bun to fuel the body. The more fresh, oxygenated air we take into the body and the more stale carbon dioxide we expel, the healthier the body is. It makes our skin glow, our hair shine, our eyes sparkle, and even puts the spring in our step. It is the single most important power source for vitality, energy, and quick thinking. But most of us only use half our lung capacity with every breath we take. At rest, we inhale approximately 15 fl oz (half a litre) of air every four to six seconds, depending on age, size, the condition of lungs, and strength of abdomen muscles.

When our bodies are under pressure and suffering from stress, this rate drops even lower. Emotions automatically affect the way we breathe; in a moment of shock we take in extra air with a deep gasp, when we are excited we switch to fast, rapidly absorbed panting. But when we are tense, our breathing becomes quick and shallow, using only the upper chest, which produces a build-up of wastes and lack of oxygen. This means that our bodies become sluggish: we are less co-ordinated, slower, sleepier, and thick-headed.

The simple solution is consciously to switch from shallow breathing to deep, slow lung-fuls of air whenever you are stressed. Although we are oblivious most of the time to our rate of breathing, it is an action that we can regulate and control, and anything that gets more air into the body, does you good. If you and your partner take a brisk 15 minute walk together, first thing in the morning or last thing at night, you will automatically increase your oxygen intake – it is impossible to exercise without breathing naturally and deeply. At the same time, you'll burn off up to 100 calories, stretch approximately 100 muscles with every stride you take, and strengthen your lungs so they work more effectively.

But you should also practise breathing properly, using your mind to correct all the bad habits that stress puts on the way our lungs function. By breathing only with the top part of the chest, we don't exchange the air sitting in the lower lungs, so it is mainly stale carbon dioxide, rather than fresh oxygen. Here is a basic energizing exercise, that you and your partner should do regularly until it becomes second nature – and then you can use it alone, in moments of stress. It also helps relax all muscles, cleanses the system, and trains you automatically to breathe in the correct, most powerful way.

HOW TO TAKE A BREATHER:

Lie comfortably on the floor in the semi-supine position (see page 113), and get your partner to place his hands across your ribcage, so his fingertips are just touching in the middle below your solar plexus (the point where the two halves of the ribcage meet). Inhale slowly and deeply through your nose, by pushing out your tummy. Hold for a count of ten, then exhale slowly and deeply by pulling your tummy down to the floor until there is no air left in your lungs. Repeat ten times, until the abdominal movement is natural and flowing. Your partner is there to check that you are really breathing to maximum capacity: if you are, his fingers should be forced apart when you inhale so there is a gap between them, and just touch again in the middle of the solar plexus when you exhale. Swap around, to see how well he breathes, and practise regularly until you can both switch to 'energy' breathing whenever you need it.

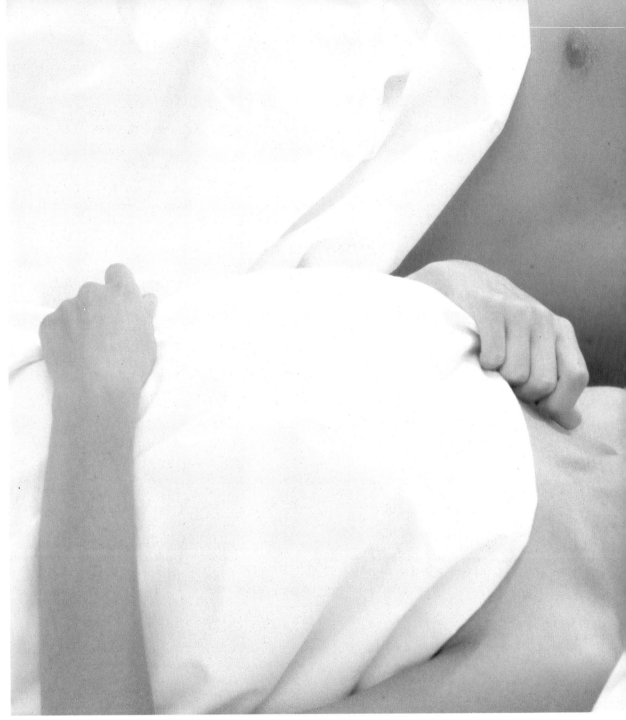

The best sleeping potion We spend about a third of our lives in oblivion – almost 25 Rip Van Winkle years, sound asleep, lying flat in bed and replaying thousands of emotional experiences in our minds that are mostly forgotten when we wake up. Some of us are sure that anything short of nine hours a night guarantees feeling like a zombie all the next day, others snatch four hours and are still up catching early-bird worms.

Many of us are forty-winkers, while a few could sleep through World War Three. But all of us use sleep time to recharge, repair, and restore our bodies and to relax and rest our minds.

When you are tense, over-stressed, and take worries to bed with you, the pattern changes. The adrenalin keeps the body tossing and the mind churning, and sleep becomes impossible. The more you try to drop off, the more anxious – and wakeful –

you become. So you try a hot milky drink, which stimulates production of relaxing hormones like serotonin, or you have a warm bath, which relaxes the muscles and quietens the mind. If you are really desperate, you take a sleeping pill, which knocks out the entire system, without giving it a chance during the night to rest naturally and re-energize. All of these things resolve the symptoms of sleeplessness, but not the source.

If you unburden your mind and muscles by consciously relaxing before you even think of sleep, you can remove the cause of insomnia.

The right sort of sleep is also extremely important. While we sleep, our minds sift, sort, and file all the day's experiences by means of dreams. If we are still tense and our minds are still active when we fall asleep, this process of refining experience cannot happen properly. Moreover, we tend to drift in and out of shallow, inadequate sleep, and wake at the slightest sound or other disturbance. By the time the morning comes, we feel like a rag – as if we have had no sleep at all. It is interesting that a total lack of sleep (at least, for one night) is often less exhausting, depriving, and depressing than having some sleep, but with the normal pattern disrupted and intermittent. (This is why new mothers find night feeds so exhausting.)

Being deeply relaxed, calm, and serene is the greatest soporific of all. If you unburden your mind and muscles before even thinking of sleep, you have removed the source of insomnia. The quickest, simplest way to relax, when you haven't the time for anything else in this book, is by using mind over matter. In only 15 minutes, you can make every part of your body – from top-to-toe – feel utterly relaxed, just by forcing muscles to let go totally. It is called conscious relaxation or visualization, and is a way of using positive thoughts with physical stretches to tense then relax every muscle group in the body.

Use it last thing at night, to prepare you for sleep while you lie snugly in bed. Bed is the one place where we all feel safe, secure, and farthest away from the pressures of the world. If your partner talks you through the routine, you can let go even more, by not having to think about what comes next. But afterwards you'll feel so serene that you won't be in the mood to reciprocate, so it is something you should take turns at on alternate nights. Whoever needs to relax most, gets first go. Once you both know the routine, you can lie close together and think it through to yourselves, so you both benefit. But many people find it most effective when they lie back and listen.

THE SLEEP TIGHT TECHNIQUE

Start off lying in bed with your eyes closed and breathe deeply and properly for a minute. Try to sink into the mattress so you give in to gravity. Then you are ready for your partner to begin working through the following steps. From now on, just do as you are told. Your partner's task is to talk you into tensing then relaxing different muscle groups, one at a time. He should feel free to improvise, so it sounds like him rather than a text book talking; these words are a guideline only.

Use a calm, soothing tone and pace each instruction so she has plenty of time to do it. Start from the top and tell her to: 'Focus on the tension in your head, face, eyes, jaw, and find the tight areas. Now let them go limp, feel the tension draining away. Tighten all the muscles, screw up your face, squeeze, and hold for a count of ten. Now slowly let go, release all the tension, feel floppy, and relaxed.'

Repeat the same procedure, thinking about the tension, making it flow away, tensing the muscles and then releasing them – only this time on the shoulder and neck area. Make her hunch her shoulders up to her ears, before she releases them, goes heavy, and gives in to the pull of gravity.

Repeat your instructions but direct them to the entire torso, tightening the chest, abdomen, and back until it is rigid, then letting go.

Make her clench her fists and feel the tension moving up her arms to her shoulders, hold and then release.

Finally, instruct her to feel the tension in her feet, moving slowly up the legs to the thighs, and let it flow away. Tense the whole area in the same order, hold for a count of ten, then relax. Now leave her to lie in this deeply relaxed, totally serene state for five minutes, before gently rousing her with a cuddle.

Glossary of further techniques

ACUPRESSURE This Eastern therapy originated in China. The fingers are used to apply pressure and stimulate specific energy points throughout the body.

ACUPUNCTURE A Chinese therapy dating back 5,000 years, acupuncture uses fine needles to puncture the skin at certain points to restore the balance of energy.

ALEXANDER TECHNIQUE A therapy pioneered by the Austrian, F. Matthias Alexander, late last century, it uses a series of postural exercises to realign the spine and correct body movements to affect overall muscle development, stance and confidence. It also helps reduce muscular pain and tension.

AROMATHERAPY A technique that stimulates the sense of smell, and treats the mind and body using powerful substances called essential oils.

BREATHING TECHNIQUES As breathing is linked to emotions and becomes faster but shallower under stress, slow, deep breathing is taught as a way of learning to relax.

CARRIER OIL Any massage oil used to dilute the potent essential oils for aromatherapy treatments. The best types include apricot kernel, avocado, grapeseed, safflower, sesame, soya, sweet almond, and sunflower.

ESSENTIAL OIL Aromatic, natural extracts from plants with properties ranging from the basic antiseptic or anti-inflammatory to powerful mood altering benefits. Pure essential oils are highly concentrated and should always be diluted before being applied to the skin.

FLOTATION TANK THERAPY A method of reaching a state of deep relaxation by lying in a dark tank of salty, buoyant water – as a brief escape from most sensory experiences.

HYDROTHERAPY Any treatments using water to increase well-being, whether internally or externally. Hydrotherapy involves dozens of techniques, including compresses, inhalation, hot and cold showers, jet sprays, baths, whirlpools, saunas, and steam rooms.

MASSAGE A relaxation technique used by many cultures throughout the world for thousands of years, it involves rubbing, kneading, and stroking the body with the hands to stimulate and soothe muscles, joints, and circulation. The commonest type is Swedish massage.

REFLEXOLOGY This technique uses massage and finger pressure to stimulate specific energy points on the soles of the feet, which restores the energy flow to organs and zones throughout the body.

ROLFING A technique pioneered in the United States 40 years ago by Dr. Ida Rolf, it involves stretching and loosening connective tissues throughout the body to realign it in its natural, correct posture.

SAUNA Similar to the Turkish bath, the sauna was developed by the Finns. It uses a small room and dry heat from a stove (not less than 100°F/38°C) to encourage perspiration, followed by a cold shower or plunge to close the pores.

SHIATSU The name comes from the Japanese: *shi*, meaning finger, and *atsu*, meaning pressure. It is a form of massage using pressure alone on various energy points along meridians associated with the function of organs throughout the body.

THALASSATHERAPY This range of treatments uses ingredients from the ocean which are rich in minerals similar to those found naturally in human blood.

VISUALIZATION THERAPY A technique to release bottled-up emotions and tensions by using the power of the mind and imagination to create positive thoughts and images. It may also be linked to conscious relaxation, where you tense and relax individual muscles to force the body to relax. It can also be combined with deep breathing techniques, as a type of meditation. Now that the power of the mind over the body is recognized by scientists, visualization is being used more and more to treat diseases.

Useful addresses

UNITED STATES

MASSAGE
American Massage Therapy Association
(AMTA)
1130 West North Avenue
Chicago, IL 60626-4670
Tel: (312) 761-2682

Boulder School of Massage Therapy
PO Box 4573
Boulder, CO 80306
Tel: (303) 443-5131

The Connecticut Center for Massage
Therapy
75 Kitts Vale
Newington, CT 06111
Tel: (203) 667-1886

The Trager Institute
300 Poplar Avenue
Suite 5
Mill Valley, CA 94941
Tel: (415) 388-2688

SHIATSU
American Shiatsu Association
PO Box 718
Jamaica Plain, MA 02130

Shiatsu Education Center
52 West 55 Street
New York, NY 10019

REFLEXOLOGY
International Institute of Reflexology
PO Box 12642
St. Petersburg, FL 33733-2642
Tel: (813) 343-4811

Laura Norman Reflexology Center
117 East 24th Street, Suite 4B
New York, NY 10010

AROMATHERAPY
American Aromatherapy Association
3949 Longridge Avenue
Sherman Oaks, CA 91423
Tel: (818) 986-0594

The International Herb Growers and
Marketers Association
The Executive Director
Maureen Buehrle
PO Box 281
Silver Spring, PA 17575
Tel: (717) 285-4252

U.K.

MASSAGE
London College of Massage,
c/o 21 Portland Place,
London,
W1N 3AF
Tel: 01-978 8150

Northern Institute of Massage,
100 Waterloo Road,
Blackpool,
Lancashire,
FY4 1AW
Tel: (0253) 403548

SHIATSU
The Shiatsu Society,
19 Langside Park,
Kilbarchan,
Renfrewshire,
PA10 2EP
Tel: (05057) 4657

REFLEXOLOGY
British School of Reflexology,
92 Sheering Road,
Old Harlow,
Essex,
CN17 0JW
Tel: (0279) 29060

The Dallamore College of Advanced
Reflexology,
9 Mead Road,
Shenley, Radlett,
Hertfordshire,
WD7 9DA
Tel: 01-450 0454 (for enquiries)

AROMATHERAPY
(E.O.T.A.) Essential Oil Traders
Association Ltd.,
Sarnett House,
Repton Drive,
Gidea Park,
Essex,
RM2 5LP
Tel: 0708 20289

International Federation of
Aromatherapists,
4 East Mearn Road,
West Dulwich,
London SE21 8HA
(SAE only)

GENERAL SOURCES OF THERAPISTS
Society for Teachers of Alexander
Technique,
Flat 10,
London House,
266 Fulham Road,
London,
SW10 9EZ

AUSTRALIA

MASSAGE
Melbourne School of Tactile Therapies,
10 Ellingworth Parade,
Box Hill,
Victoria 3128
Tel: (03) 890 5599 (or 898 4930 after hours)

Naturecare School of Remedial
Therapies,
1a Frederick Street,
Artarmon,
Sydney,
Tel: (02) 439 8844

SHIATSU
East West Centre,
215a Thomas Street,
Haymarket, Sydney,
Tel: (02) 212 4177

Sydney Shiatsu College,
215a Thomas Street,
Haymarket,
New South Wales 2000
Tel: (02) 212 3616

AROMATHERAPY
Association of Aromatherapists,
693 Rathdowne Street,
Carlton,
Victoria 3053
Tel: (03) 817 6431

Australian Plantation Products,
The Chairman,
Stanley Coupe,
280 Pacific Highway,
Lindfield,
New South Wales 2070
Tel: (612) 437 4955

GENERAL SOURCES OF THERAPISTS
Natural Therapists Association,
P.O. Box 522
Sutherland,
Sydney,
New South Wales 2232
Tel: (02) 521 2063 or 521 5212

The Yoga Centre,
1st Floor,
14 Thomas Street,
Chatswood,
Sydney
Tel: (02) 43 2657

NEW ZEALAND

The New Zealand Natural Health
Practitioners Accreditation Board Inc,
c/o South Pacific College of Natural
Therapeutics,
PO Box 11–311,
Auckland
Tel: (09) 594997

Index

Abdomen 25, 26, 49, 102, 109, 127, 137, 140
Allergy 20, 99
Almond 76
Ankle 19, 22, 43, 44, 45, 48, 49, 102, 125, 126, 130, 136
Anxiety 11, 14, 17, 62, 63, 66, 67, 73, 90, 116
Apricot 76
Aquarobics 87, 90
Arm 22, 33, 36, 40, 41, 48, 49, 102, 108, 109, 122, 123, 126, 127, 129, 130, 140
Aromatherapy 14, 24, 56–74, 93, 97, 109
–oil see Essential oil
Avocado 76

Back 19, 25, 28, 32, 33, 35, 38–41, 48, 72, 78, 102, 104, 109, 121, 125, 129, 130, 140
Bath 18, 24, 69, 70, 74, 76, 80, 88, 93, 94–6, 97–9, 101–3, 104, 109, 115, 139
Beauty aids 74–80, 90
Body brush, Dry 102, 109
Body press 24, 121–3
Body wrapping 90, 93
Buttocks 25, 28, 29, 33, 40, 41, 48, 49, 102, 108, 125, 130

Camomile 74, 76
Chest 33, 35, 48, 49, 102, 108, 109, 121, 123, 125, 126, 127, 129, 130, 131, 140
Cucumber 78

Depression 62, 73, 116
Dreams 84, 140

Essential oil 20, 33, 56, 59, 60, 62–7, 68, 69–74, 81, 94, 96, 97–9, 102, 132, 134, 135, 136
Exercise 87, 90, 106–9, 112, 118, 121–31

Face 25, 32, 33, 35–7, 43, 70, 76, 78, 80, 87, 92, 140
Facial 90, 93
Fango 92
Fig 76, 78
Foot 22, 25, 32, 33, 41, 43–5, 48, 49, 69, 70, 80, 92, 102, 125, 127, 129, 130, 132, 134, 136, 140
Footbath 93, 132, 134

Hair 33, 35, 36, 37, 53, 64, 67, 72, 76, 78, 92, 104, 137
Hand 11, 14, 20, 22, 24, 25, 28, 29, 30, 31, 33, 35, 36, 37, 40, 41, 44, 45, 48, 49, 78, 104, 109, 121, 122, 123, 126, 127, 130,
131, 134, 135–6
Head 19, 35, 36, 38, 40, 104, 121, 126, 129, 130, 140
Heel 44, 45, 48, 130, 136
Herbs 56, 58, 59, 81, 90, 97
–tea 81
Hip 40, 41, 48, 49, 102, 126, 130
Honey 78, 81

Insomnia 14, 67, 81, 140

Knee 19, 22, 44, 48, 49, 80, 102, 109, 125, 126, 127, 129, 130, 131

Laughter 112, 116–18
Leg 25, 26, 33, 35, 41, 43, 44, 49, 102, 108, 109, 125, 126, 129, 130, 131, 140
Lemon 76, 78, 134, 135
Libido, Loss of 62, 67, 73
Manicure 76, 78, 92, 134, 135–6
Massage 11, 12, 13, 14–49, 60, 69, 70–3, 76, 80, 92, 96, 101, 103, 104, 115, 132, 134, 135
–basic strokes 17, 22, 26, 28–31
–and childbirth 25
–contra-indications 25
–oil 18, 20, 26, 35, 37, 40, 43, 44, 48, 49, 70, 72, 73, 76, 135, 136
–step-by-step 32–49, 72–3
Mood 53, 72, 73, 94
Mud 92, 97
Muscle 14–17, 18, 19, 22, 24, 25, 26, 29, 30, 31, 35, 40, 41, 43, 62, 63, 66, 67, 87, 101, 102, 104, 106, 109, 113, 116, 118, 122, 123, 124, 126, 127, 129, 130, 131, 132, 134, 137, 139, 140

Neck 25, 32, 33, 35–7, 48, 49, 72, 92, 95, 102, 104, 121, 122, 133, 140

Oatmeal 78
Orange 11, 60, 78

Papaya 80, 134
Peach 74, 80
Pedicure 80, 92, 134, 136
Potato 74, 76, 80
Pregnancy 25, 62, 64, 87

Reflexology 14, 32–3, 132
Relaxation 26, 33, 35, 36, 62, 63, 66, 67, 73, 74, 90, 92, 99, 112, 113, 115, 116, 118, 121, 129, 130, 140

Salt rub 102–3, 109, 132, 134
Sauna 74, 92, 93

Scalp 25, 32, 33, 35–7, 72, 76, 104, 121, 122
Scotch douche 92
Sea kelp 80
Seaweed 93, 97
Sensuality 11, 13, 18, 20, 22, 25, 26, 32, 33, 35, 43, 46–9, 63, 70, 72–3, 87, 99, 104, 106, 132
Sexuality 11, 25, 46, 52, 53, 84
Shiatsu 14, 32, 137
Shoulder 19, 25, 28, 29, 35, 36, 40, 41, 48, 49, 102, 104, 108, 109, 121, 122, 123, 126, 127, 129, 130, 131, 140
Shower 92–3, 95, 101, 104
Sitz bath 93
Skin 8, 10, 11, 14, 17, 20, 22, 24, 25, 28, 30, 31, 33, 36, 37, 40, 43, 46, 49, 62, 63, 64, 66, 67, 70, 72, 74, 76, 78, 80, 82, 87, 90, 92, 101, 102, 104, 134, 135, 137
Sleep 18, 20, 24, 53, 64, 76, 81, 110, 112, 138–40
Smell 50–81, 87, 97, 98, 99
Spa 12–13, 88, 90–3, 102
Spine 19, 24, 25, 29, 31, 38, 40, 41, 104, 109, 121, 123
Steam therapies 93
Strawberry 74, 80
Stress 14, 17, 35, 53, 63, 66, 67, 70, 90, 96, 104, 112, 113–15, 116, 118, 124, 132, 137, 139
Swedish massage 32–3
Swimming pool 93, 106–9

Taste 52, 53
Tea, Herbal 81
Tension 11, 17, 22, 25, 26, 29, 35, 40, 43, 52, 64, 66, 70, 104, 113, 118, 121, 124, 129, 130, 137, 139, 140
Thigh 43, 48, 49, 102, 108, 109, 125, 126, 127, 140
Ticklishness 22, 24, 29, 43, 102, 116
Toe 44, 45, 109, 136
Tomato 80
Touch 8, 10, 11, 13, 17, 22, 24, 32, 35, 46, 48, 49, 50, 52, 60, 69
Turkish bath 93

Vitamins 11, 20, 58, 64, 70, 76, 78, 80

Waist 19, 25, 28, 40, 41, 48, 49, 102, 104, 108, 109, 121, 130
Water 20, 56, 69, 73, 74, 82–109, 110, 118, 132, 137
–exercise 87, 90, 106–9
Watermelon 80
Whirlpool 93